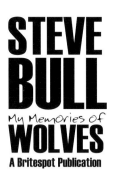

STEVE
BULL
My Memories of
WOLVES
A Britespot Publication

*Dedicated
to my sons Jack and Joe*

Dennis Westcott (l) and Tom Galley (r)

Introduction

GOLDEN BOOTS
In the footsteps of great strikers

Molineux was a ramshackle old place by the time Steve Bull joined Wolves, but he was well aware he was stepping into a football ground which was steeped in tradition.

Wolverhampton Wanderers was in a state of decay in November 1986, with two sides of Molineux closed for safety reasons and the other two stands perfectly adequate to house the sparse crowds who turned up to watch a team languishing in the lower reaches of the old Fourth Division.

But the stories those rusty, run-down buildings could tell! Three decades earlier the place had reverberated to the sound of 55,000 supporters roaring on the mighty Wolves in their famous floodlit friendlies against European giants Moscow Dynamo, Honved and Spartak Moscow before the men in gold and black celebrated two consecutive League championship triumphs.

And while the glory days had long since gone, Bully knew he was following in the footsteps of some of the finest goalscorers in football history.

As far back as 1877, the year of Wolves' formation under the name St Luke's, the club had boasted a prolific marksman. Not only was Jack Brodie one of the club's founder members, along with Jack Addenbrooke and goalkeeper John Baynton, he was also a footballer who could play in any forward position. His powerful shot brought him 44 goals in 65 games – plus three England caps – during those pioneering years before he retired in 1891 in the knowledge that Wolves were firmly established as members of the Football League.
Two years after Brodie's departure, the club won the FA Cup for the first time, beating Everton 1-0 with the help of two of the men who had taken over his goalscoring mantle.

Walsall-born Harry Wood, who was also capped three times by his country, had the distinction of being the first man to reach a century of competitive goals for Wolves. Wood's tally over two spells with the club was 126, a figure which would surely have been matched by David Wykes had the talented inside-forward not been struck down by typhoid fever and pneumonia at the age of 28.
Wykes, who was on target 69 times in 179 appearances, died in October, 1895, just 24 hours after playing for Wolves against Stoke City.

Wolves were also FA Cup runners-up in 1889 – the year they moved to Molineux – and 1896, and they enjoyed their second triumph in 1908 with a 3-1 victory over Newcastle United at Crystal Palace. At the time, Wolves were ninth in Division Two, and they remain the lowest-placed club ever to have lifted the Cup.
Their team that day included two more hot-shots, Billy Wooldridge and George Hedley, scorers of 81 and 74 goals respectively during their Molineux careers, but it would be a number of years before the next great striker emerged.

Tom Phillipson spent five years with Wolves from 1923, and produced an incredible ratio – 111 goals in 159 games – as well as once scoring in 13 consecutive league matches.
And as Phillipson departed in 1928, into the breach stepped Billy Hartill, a man who was on target a total of 170 times and who set a club record of 162 league goals which stood until Steve Bull came along.

Bully also surpassed Dennis Wescott's record of 43 League and cup goals in one season, although he just missed out on Westcott's incredible haul of 38 League goals in one campaign, falling just one short of the target when Wolves were promoted as Third Division champions in 1988-89.
Westcott, in fairness, achieved his feat in the top flight, during the first post-war season of League football.
A member of the side beaten by Portsmouth in the 1939 Cup Final – Wolves' first Wembley appearance – Westcott boasted a return of 124 goals in 144 games, and may well have set an unassailable target had the hostilities with Germany not robbed him of the best years of his career.

John Richards

He eventually left to join Blackburn Rovers in 1948, by which time Jesse Pye had arrived on the Molineux scene.
Signed from Notts County, Pye scored 95 goals during his six-year Wolves career, including two in the 1949 Cup Final victory over Leicester City.

Next up were two more centurions. Dennis Wilshaw, who graduated through the club's youth ranks, netted a hat-trick on his debut against Newcastle in March, 1949 and went on to accumulate 117 goals in 232 appearances until his departure to Stoke City eight years later.
Both Wilshaw and Roy Swinbourne were members of the Wolves' team who won the Championship for the first time in 1953-54 and finished runners-up a year later, and their careers ran parallel in other ways, too.
Swinbourne, big, strong and skilful, also made his debut in 1949, and his goal haul was 114 in 230 games before his career was curtailed by a serious knee injury in 1957, the year Wilshaw headed for fresh pastures in the Potteries.

Four other players also contributed significantly to Wolves' goal haul throughout the fifties, even though none was a striker in the recognised sense of the word.
Peter Broadbent, a majestic inside-forward who was the architect of so many goals for team-mates, also found time to score 145 himself in a wonderful Molineux career which included three Championships – 1954, 1958 and 1959 – plus the 1960 FA Cup triumph over Blackburn Rovers.
And in those days of flying wingers, no-one could complain about the input of Johnny Hancocks (168 in 378 games), Jimmy Mullen (112 in 486) and Norman Deeley (73 in 237).

Swinbourne's successor as centre-forward, though, was even more prolific than that quartet of marksman. In contrast to the powerful Swinbourne, Jimmy Murray was neat and elusive, his return of 166 goals in 299 games indicating just how frequently he escaped defenders' clutches.

After the fabulous fifties, sadly, the early sixties brought a decline in Wolves' fortunes, culminating in relegation in 1965, but they were back two years later as another lethal marksman was recruited. Derek Dougan, who had played for Blackburn against Wolves in the 1960 Cup Final, was signed from Leicester during the run-in to promotion and by the time he retired in 1975, the flamboyant Irishman had netted 123 times in 323 games.

That, though, was nothing by comparison with John Richards, who initially forged a productive partnership with 'The Doog' and continued banging in the goals long after his colleague's retirement.
Richards scored the winner in the 1974 League Cup final victory over Manchester City and was also in the side who beat Nottingham Forest 1-0 in the 1980, when Scottish striker Andy Gray hit the only goal.

Richards set new standards in goalscoring for Wolves, his 486 appearances producing a record 194 which many people were convinced would never be bettered. Steve Bull had other ideas...

Chairman Sir Jack Hayward OBE

FOREWORD
by Sir Jack Hayward OBE

To have been asked to write this Foreword to Steve's book is indeed an honour, for to have known Steve and seen him perform his deeds for our beloved Wolves has been a great privilege in my life.

There is no need here to go into the many feats and records achieved by Steve. All these are recorded in the book you are about to read.

I can sum up Steve's association with Wolves by stating without any fear of contradiction that his service to Wolverhampton Wanderers is the primary reason the club is now in the First Division and fighting to get into the Premier League. Steve and his fellow team mates are responsible for bringing our great club up from the depths of the old Fourth Division to where we are today.

Steve Bull must now surely rank alongside the many great and illustrious players who have illuminated the Molineux pitch and thrilled the most loyal fans in Great Britain.

Lucky as I am, it is within my power to honour Steve as I (and so many other fans) feel is his due.

With his agreement and permission my colleagues at Wolves and I would like, at the start of next season, to re-name the present John Ireland Stand The Steve Bull Stand.

Sir Jack Hayward OBE
Pitcairn Island, March 7, 2003

In action against Burnley in the Sherpa Van Trophy Final, Wembley, 29 May 1988

STEVE BULL
My Memories of
WOLVES

My Memories of Wolves by Steve Bull
A Britespot Publication

First Published in Great Britain by
Britespot Publishing Solutions Limited
Chester Road, Cradley Heath, West Midlands B64 6AB

© Britespot April 2003

ISBN 1 904103 07 3

Cover design and layout
© Britespot Publishing Solutions Limited

Printed and bound in Great Britain by
The Cromwell Press,
Aintree Avenue,
White Horse Business Park,
Trowbridge,
Wiltshire,
BA14 OXB

Steve Bull would like to thank:
Roger Marshall, Paul Burns, Linda Perkins, Darren Cartwright and Rachel Burns of Britespot Publishing for making the publishing of this book possible. Sid Day, Nobby Stiles, Sir Jack for his kind words, Graham Turner for believing in me and all those at WWFC who have helped me with my career. Mom and Dad for always being there and Kirsty for her support, now and in the future. Last but not least a big thank you to all my fans who have braved the weather, the good times and the bad times for all those years.
Thank you everyone. I could not have done it without you.

The publisher would like to thank:
Rob Bishop and Geoff Coleman who have helped with the compilation of this publication,
James Cadman for helping develop the concept and Tony Matthews for the goal by goal statistics.

Photos © Action Images, Colorsport, Empics, Express & Star, PA Sport.

A photocall at the beginning of the 1990/91 Season, Barclays League Division Two

CONTENTS
Chapters

Scotland's Maurice Malpas climbs above me to head clear in the Rous Cup, 27th May 1989

Chapter 1

BLACK COUNTRY ROUTE
From the Lost City to Molineux

They called it the Lost City, the place where I grew up. It was a vast council estate which had a reputation as one of the roughest in the West Midlands. But that never bothered me. I enjoyed my childhood, and the Ocker Hill area of Tipton was where I first kicked a football.

I was actually born a mile or so away, at Leabrook Road, on March 28th, 1965, but three years later my family moved to South Road, on the Lost City.
Despite the estate's reputation, it was a safe place for us kids to play - most of the time, anyway. I had a bike which had no brakes, and one day I was taking a lemonade bottle back to the local fish and chip shop. I had the bottle tucked down the front of my jumper, but suddenly I had to stop. I put my foot on the front tyre and flew straight over the handlebars. The bottle smashed, but amazingly I didn't have a single cut. Unfortunately I didn't get 10p off the bottle, either!

"There was a wall opposite our house and I used to kick a ball against it, dreaming I was playing for England"

If I was often getting into scrapes, though, I loved playing football from as long ago as I can remember. There was a wall opposite our house and I used to kick a ball against it, dreaming I was playing for England. Sometimes, my mates joined in and we played two against two, or even one against one if there were only a couple of us, and whenever anyone scored, we used to scream "Goal!" at the top of our voices.
After a while, I joined in games with some of the bigger kids, who played on a grassed island in the middle of South Road. It was usually six-a-side, but the numbers depended of whose mothers would let them come out and play. As soon as any of our mates came out of the front door, we called them over for a game. To be honest, we weren't very well organised. We threw our coats or jumpers down for goalposts, and everyone ran all over the place because we just wanted to get the ball. But those were great times - and there was even a lamp post which acted as our floodlights when it got dark!

When I was a bit older, we took our ball over the park for a game, but sometimes my mates wouldn't let me join in with them. They said I was too selfish and I suppose they were right - I always wanted to score rather than pass the ball! Then I took a fancy to being a goalkeeper, because I loved diving all over the place and getting my trousers dirty. But the other lads weren't keen on that because they said I was too small.
I suppose my tiny frame as a kid was one of the reasons I was a late developer as a footballer, but I started to play more often after I went to the Willingsworth senior school.
That was where I should have got myself some qualifications, but the only thing which really interested me was the competition we held every afternoon when the final bell went - to see who was first over the park with a ball!

In those early days, I played for a number of teams apart from the school sides. There was the Princes End Colts, then Bustleholme Boys - where I usually had to settle for being substitute - and later Newey Goodman, who were one of the top Sunday clubs in the area.
But my real break came when a guy called Sid Day, who ran Tipton Town's youth team, spotted me playing for Willingsworth High School. His house was near the school and he watched me in action one day when he was walking his dog. I used to deliver his papers and he kept telling me he would give me a game when I was a bit older.
He kept his word, too. When I was 14, I played for Tipton youths in division five of the Sandwell Sunday League, and I gradually progressed to the reserves and then the first team, who played in the West Midlands League.

Steve Bull, West Bromwich Albion 1986

Although a lot of non-League clubs paid their players a few pounds expenses, Tipton couldn't afford it, but that never bothered me. I just wanted to play football, either for Tipton on Saturday afternoons or Neweys on Sunday mornings.

I'd also had a few jobs by then. When I left school I worked for a bed manufacturing company called Vono, screwing and gluing the ends and sides of beds together for £27 a week. After that I was a fork-lift truck driver for a building supplies company, before working in a warehouse, stacking packs of fasteners.

It was while I was in that job that Sid Day got me fixed up with West Bromwich Albion on a week-to-week arrangement. I owe Sid a lot, because that got me started in professional football, but it took quite a while before Albion decided to sign me on a proper contract. At first, I just trained whenever I could and played for the third team on Saturday mornings. Then I started to get the odd game for the reserves in midweek, but not before I'd put in a full shift at work!

By the time Albion decided to take me on, I had turned 20. Nobby Stiles, one of England's 1966 World Cup heroes, was Albion's youth team coach at the time, and he recommended to manager Johnny Giles that I was worth a contract because of my goalscoring potential. Thankfully I proved the point a few days later by scoring against Everton in a reserve match.

Nobby was a big help in my development because he insisted that I worked hard in training and learned discipline. He was also the man who gave me my first team debut - after he had taken over as caretaker manager - in a Full Members Cup-tie against Crystal Palace on Wednesday 23rd October, 1985.

Fewer than 4,000 people turned up at The Hawthorns that night, but that didn't matter to me as I went on as a second half substitute for Garth Crooks and we won 2-1.

Not long afterwards, I was sub again when we played Chelsea in the quarter-finals and that night I scored my first goal in senior professional football - a penalty in a shoot-out which we lost 5-4. But I had quite a wait for my next game in the first team.

It turned out to be my only appearance in English football's top flight, a 24-minute outing as substitute in a 1-0 defeat by QPR at Loftus Road on Saturday 12th April, 1986.

By then, Nobby had left the club and Ron Saunders had taken over as manager. The former Aston Villa and Birmingham City boss had a reputation as a hard taskmaster, but he never said a great deal to me. He once had a go at me about what I was eating and drinking because he said I was overweight, but I can't remember many other conversations with him.

"Little could I have known that a move across the Black Country was about to open up a new road for me..."

At the start of the following season I finally started an Albion match at Reading when the club's new signing Stewart Evans was suspended, and I followed up by scoring twice in a 4-3 home defeat by Ipswich the following Saturday. Even though we lost, it was a tremendous feeling to score two goals, and I also got one when we were beaten at Derby in the League Cup a few days later.

But it was clear that Saunders didn't have a lot of time for me and I only played a couple more matches for the first team after that, being substituted on both occasions.

Then it was back to the reserves, and suddenly my career seemed to be going nowhere. Little could I have known that even though I was running into a dead end at West Brom, a move across the Black Country was about to open up a new road for me...

WOLVES £70,000 SWOOP

By MIKE WARD

Wolves today lashed out £70,000 for West Bromwich Albion youngsters Steve Bull and Andy Thompson as Albion prepared to sell Craig Madden to Blackpool.

On a day of hectic transfer dealings at both clubs, Wolves spent £50,000 on the tall, 23-year-old striker Bull and around £20,000 for teenage midfielder Thompson.

Personal terms had already been agreed and the transfer was going through subject to the routine medicals.

Bull and Thompson are in line for their debuts at home to Wrexham on Saturday.

Wolves failed in an ambitious bid to sign Watford's Les Taylor but manager Graham Turner said: "We are delighted with this double investment, which we are confident will bring an excellent return.

"Above all, we have shown the supporters that we have a board who are prepared to back the club with the necessary cash to strengthen the team."

Madden was poised to leave The Hawthorns only eight months and nine appearances after joining Albion in a £50,000 move from Bury.

Albion were hoping to recoup at least what they paid for the 28-year-old striker, who has failed to reproduce the form which earned him 297 goals in 129 League games for Third Division Bury.

Crooks staying

One striker staying at The Hawthorns is Garth Crooks. Manager Ron Saunders revealed today that he had come off the transfer list after re-establishing himself in the first-team.

The last time Wolves spent any significant amount was two years ago when they paid Ipswich £35,000 for defender David Barnes.

All dealings were suspended when Wolves went into receivership for the second time.

Young Albion pair signed

Andy Thompson: £20,000 signing.

Albion manager Ron Saunders was hoping to use that money in the transfer market, along with the cash had raised from yesterday's double sales of Andy Thompson and Steve Bull to Wolves.

Despite missing out a Madden transfer, Saunders today confirmed that he was still in the market to make a signing.

"I am always looking for players," he said.

Earlier in the season he made an inquiry after Port Vale's midfielder Geoff Hunter. Vale manager John Rudge today confirmed the clubs had discussed the possibility of a swop deal involving Bull.

Those plans went out of the window yesterday however when Bull moved to Wolves. Saunders is expected to keep a close eye on the Port Vale situation, however with transfer-listed Hunter looking for a move from Vale Park.

Meantime, Saunders is preparing his side for tomorrow's Second Division clash with Millwall.

He has injury worries, and will name the side which went down 1-0 at Plymouth last Saturday, with the sub not being announced until just before the k...

Madd £40,000 transfer al off

s Sunday

adden's l fell hen not terms Division

d agreed a fee, to be around

Chapter 2

A TRANSFER RECORD?
The day I signed

It always amazes me when I hear about transfer deals which drag on for weeks, or sometimes even months. When I joined Wolves from West Bromwich Albion, the whole business took just five hours!

Looking back, it seems incredible that a transfer between two major clubs should be completed in such a short space of time, but I suppose the circumstances played a major part. Albion were quite happy to let me go and Wolves desperately needed a striker to try and lift them away from the bottom end of the old Fourth Division, so it was merely a question of the clubs agreeing a fee.

Things have changed a fair bit in the financial respect, too. These days, even ordinary footballers tend to cost at least £1m, but the figure agreed between the two old Black Country rivals for my services was £54,000 - plus an extra £5,000 to be paid when I'd played 20 games and a further £5,000 when I reached 40 appearances in gold and black. Without being big-headed, I reckon I gave a pretty good return on the investment!

At the time, of course, you could understand why Wolves weren't going to break the bank to get me. Although I'd played briefly in the top flight, as well as turning out for Albion in a few cup matches, there was no cast iron guarantee I would be the answer to the problems at Molineux.

The majority of my goals had been scored either in non-League football or for Albion's reserves, which didn't automatically mean I was about to terrorise defenders who had been brought up in the professional game.

But Wolves' chief scout Ron Jukes had watched me several times in the Central League, and he told manager Graham Turner I might just be the man to launch a Molineux revival. Actually, Ron and Graham decided it might take two new men, which is why they also signed another Albion player, midfielder Andy Thompson, on the same day - Thursday 20th November, 1986.

"It was obvious I wasn't wanted at The Hawthorns"

I'll never forget the events of that day. When we turned up for training at Albion's old Spring Road training ground, Andy was told by chief scout Norman Bodell to get himself off to The Hawthorns, where manager Ron Saunders wanted to speak to him.

Not long afterwards, I was given the same message by Keith Leonard, another member of the Baggies' backroom staff, and although I didn't realise it, the double transfer was under way. I must admit that when Andy went off to the ground to see the manager, I thought he might be leaving, but I never imagined it would be me as well.

Andy came out of the manager's office just as I was going in, and Saunders joked that Halifax Town had come in for me! Then he told me he had accepted a £50,000 offer from Wolves, and I couldn't quite believe it. My first thought was that I just wasn't worth that much, and it certainly seemed to be a lot of money for anyone to be paying for a reserve player.

Albion had been relegated the previous season, but Saunders made it quite clear he didn't think my touch was good enough, even for the old Second Division. Then he suggested I should think seriously about going to Wolves. To be honest, that more or less made up my mind, because it was obvious I wasn't wanted at The Hawthorns.

What I didn't realise was that Saunders hadn't totally written me off as a no-hoper. While he didn't see me as part of his plans for Albion, there was obviously a nagging doubt that he might be losing someone capable of knocking in a goal or two. That's the only reason I can imagine that he insisted on a sell-on clause which ensured Albion of 30 per cent of the profit if Wolves decided to sell me.

STEVE
BULL
The Movie of
WOLVES

Photocall for the 1988/89 Season

Once my meeting with Saunders was over, Andy and I drove over to Molineux to discuss personal terms, and although we didn't really know each other that well, we suddenly realised we had something very important in common. On the way to Wolverhampton we talked things over, and decided that if we were made decent offers, we would both sign. I went in first, and was happy with what they offered, so after about five minutes the deal was done and I was a Wolves player.

As I came out of the boardroom, I told Andy I had signed. Then he went in, and got sorted out even quicker than me - probably no more than three minutes, I'd say. It was as simple as that.

Once the business had been completed, Andy and I headed home, while Graham Turner and Ron Jukes drove to The Hawthorns to get the forms signed by Albion chairman Sid Lucas. If Andy and I were to make our debuts against Wrexham two days later, our transfers had to be lodged with the Football League by 5pm that afternoon.

"After about five minutes the deal was done and I was a Wolves player"

I didn't realise it at the time, but I'm told that between Graham telephoning Ron Saunders to make his double offer, and the paperwork being registered with the League, took just five hours. The fees may not have been records, but it's hard to imagine any transfer deal in the future happening quite as quickly!

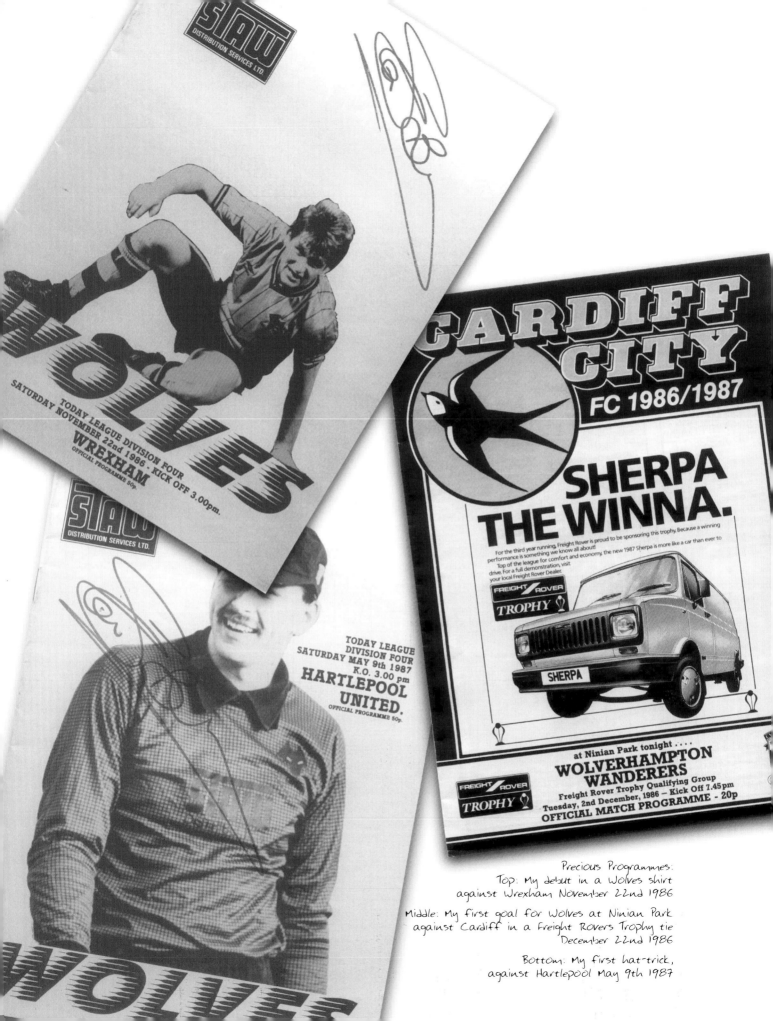

Precious Programmes.
Top: My debut in a Wolves shirt against Wrexham November 22nd 1986

Middle: My first goal for Wolves at Ninian Park against Cardiff in a Freight Rovers Trophy tie December 22nd 1986

Bottom: My first hat-trick, against Hartlepool May 9th 1987

Chapter 3

GOING UP, GOING UP
Promotion at the double

Here's a confession for you. Within a few days of signing for Wolves, I started to wonder if I'd dropped a real clanger. When I moved to Molineux, I thought I was aware of how badly the club were struggling, but within four days of my arrival I realised that things were much worse than I'd imagined.

My debut, against Wrexham on the Saturday after my transfer, brought only a 3-0 home defeat, and I can't remember too much about the game, apart from the fact that Wrexham had a really big guy in defence. I was anxious to show I was worth the money Wolves had paid for me, but he obviously did a good job in keeping me quiet.

But that was nothing compared with the depression I experienced at Bolton's Burnden Park just over 48 hours later, when Wolves played Chorley in an FA Cup second replay. The teams had already drawn twice, which was obviously an embarrassment for a club with as big a name as Wolverhampton Wanderers, but when they lost 3-0 to the non-Leaguers at Bolton it was humiliating.

Myself and Andy Thompson weren't eligible for the tie, so we watched from the stand - and I'm sure anyone who was there that night will tell you it was abysmal. Andy and I wondered what we had let ourselves in for, and it even crossed my mind that I might have been better off staying with Albion!

It didn't make much difference when Andy and I were back in the side the following Saturday as we lost 3-0 at Lincoln. But at least we managed to stop the rot in the next match, a Freight Rover Trophy tie at Cardiff. We won 1-0 at Ninian Park and I scored my first goal in the famous gold shirt.

The game seemed to be heading for a goalless draw, but 15 minutes from time I went up for a high ball with one of their defenders. As the ball dropped, I tried to get in a shot and my finger went in the lad's eye. It was an accident, but I realised I had the chance to score so I just hit the ball as hard as I could.

I then scored my first League goal for Wolves in a 1-0 win at Hartlepool, but although I started to form an effective partnership with Andy Mutch at that time, it wasn't until February that our season really started to take off.

In the final 19 matches, we lost only twice and at one stage we reeled off eight straight wins, which was enough to earn us fourth place and involvement in the first-ever play-offs.

Unfortunately, after beating Colchester in the semi-finals, we lost 3-0 on aggregate to an Aldershot side who had finished nine points behind us and who, of course, are no longer even a League club. But while we were bitterly disappointed at missing out on promotion, that late run gave us the belief that we could do it the following season - and what a season it turned out to be!

Apart from the fact that we went up as champions, finishing five points clear of Cardiff City, I enjoyed the sort of season I'd always dreamed about. While Wolves made football history by becoming the first team to win all four divisions, I scored a record 52 goals, 12 of them in the Sherpa Van Trophy.

My abiding memory from the start of that glorious 1987-88 season, though, is of the mindless violence which took place during our opening day match at Scarborough, who had just become the first club to be promoted from the Conference. We drew 2-2 and I scored our first goal of the season, but the crowd trouble was really frightening.

One guy fell through the roof of the stand and seemed to bounce two feet off the floor. Then people started kicking him and everyone thought he must be dead. Thankfully he was okay, and although his neck was in plaster when we saw him after the match, all he was worried about was where his fags were!

I scored a dozen times in the first 15 league and cup matches and there was talk of big clubs coming in for me, but Graham Turner wasn't interested. He made the point that Wolves were ambitious and didn't intend to sell their best players.

Even so, we weren't exactly setting the Fourth Division on fire - until we went to Carlisle in October, that is. I scored the only goal in a 1-0 win, and that started a run of 20 matches in which we were beaten only once.

Me and Phil Robinson celebrate with Andy Mutch on his goal against Burnley in the Sherpa Van trophy Final at Wembley on the 29th May 1988

You could sense that the fans believed in us, too. The crowds at Molineux had been pitiful when I joined, but our home attendances were now three or four times higher than anywhere else in Division Four.

The goals kept coming for me, too, and I broke Dennis Westcott's post-war record of 39 in one season with a hat-trick in a 5-3 home win over Darlington. That took me to 41, and Wescott's all-time record of 43, which had stood since 1938-39, was within sight. I passed it by scoring at Burnley the following Saturday and getting both goals in our 2-0 home win over Colchester on Easter Monday.

We were really flying now, and we clinched promotion with a 3-1 win at Newport County at the end of April. I reached the 50 mark at Somerton Park, and it didn't bother me that both my goals were tap-ins. All that mattered was that we were up. We lost 4-2 at Wrexham in our next match - they were our bogey team in the Fourth Division - but two more goals from Yours Truly in a 2-0 Molineux win against Hartlepool took my haul to 52 and meant we were going up as champions.

But who could have imagined that 12 months later we would be celebrating another championship and I would have scored another half century of goals? Our Third Division title success in 1988-89 was even more emphatic than the one before - this time we finished six points clear - and even though we lost our opening match at Bury, it soon became evident that we were promotion material for the second year running as we reeled off win after win.

Even so, things didn't go so well for me during the first few weeks. I'd set myself a target of 25 goals for the season, and although I scored twice in a League Cup tie against Birmingham, I didn't manage to find the net in any of our first four league games. I had plenty of chances, but it seemed the 'keeper was always in the right place. It was the worst spell I'd known and I admit it started to get me down a bit. I just kept thinking: "I'm due a goal today."

Thankfully, it finally came along when I hit the winner against Aldershot in our fifth league match, and after that I was flying. That winter, it seemed like I just couldn't stop scoring. I hit four against Preston, four against Port Vale in the Sherpa Van Trophy and hat-tricks against Mansfield, Fulham and Bury as we stormed towards the title.

We finally clinched promotion on the May Bank Holiday Monday, even though we couldn't celebrate straight after our 2-0 home win over Bristol City. I got both goals that day, but it wasn't until later in the evening, when promotion contenders Port Vale lost at home to Northampton, that our place in the Second Division was assured.

But there was better to come. We beat Northampton in the next match, and when Sheffield United came to Molineux the following Tuesday, we knew a point would make us champions.

The Blades had the same target, too, knowing that a draw would earn them automatic promotion along with us, and that's how it turned out. I put us in front with a header - my 50th Wolves goal of the season - and although Sheffield then scored twice in quick succession, Robbie Dennison's free-kick brought the scores level at 2-2.

At the end, everbody had something to celebrate, but don't get the idea that we tried to engineer a draw. Although we only needed a point, there was no question of settling for a draw. That wouldn't have been fair on Port Vale, who were also looking to get up automatically.

In any case, there was always a competitive attitude in our dressing room and before the match we desperately wanted to win the match and make United sweat for a bit longer!

As it was, they earned their point in a great game and went up with us, but I bet they didn't savour the moment quite as much as we did.

Only two-and-a-half years earlier, Wolves had faced the grim prospect of going out of business. Now we were heading for the Second Division. I hadn't dropped a clanger after all!

I celebrate the goal that gave me the all time goalscoers record against Derby County on 21st March 1992

Chapter 4

AIMING FOR THE TOP
1989 until retirement

When I look at the period from 1989 to my retirement ten years later, the overriding factor has to be that we didn't quite finish the job started by Graham Turner. We couldn't get Wolves into the Premier League, though we came bloody close more than once.

And as Molineux again became a top stadium, thanks to Sir Jack Hayward, we produced some magic moments to grace our revamped home.

"The big question was whether we could get into the top flight at the first time of asking"

After successive promotions, expectations were high as we went into the 1989/1990 season. The big question was whether we could do it again and get into the top flight at the first time of asking.

Paul Cook came in to give us a bit more craft in midfield and you'd have to say we had a decent season. But we ran out of steam and, after going into the last two months in fourth place, we ended up well off the pace in tenth.

I carried on scoring and hit 27 goals - enough to earn a place in Bobby Robson's World Cup squad - and my highlight probably came on New Year's Day at Newcastle, when I scored all four goals in a 4-1 win.

It was just one of those afternoons when everything went right. The Wolves fans were out in force in their Santa outfits, reindeer outfits, the lot. About four or five planes went up there and we repaid them with a great win. It was 0-0 at half-time and I think Mark McGhee actually missed a sitter for them just before the break. We came out in the second-half and again I scored all four goals in a 4-1 win.

Even now, when I bump into Wolves fans, that's the one game I can guarantee they'll mention. I don't know how many people were up there, but it was the perfect way to start a year. They'll never forget it and neither will I.

I didn't get as many goals that year as I had in the promotion seasons, but I don't think 27 is too bad for a striker. I always think a striker scoring between 20 and 30 goals is just what a team needs and if another player can then pop up with 15 to 20, you're well on your way.

So personally I felt it was a good season, but it was just a shame we couldn't make it three promotions in a row.

One consolation of course came with a place in Bobby Robson's World Cup squad. Just as it had been with Wolves, it was another case of so near, yet so far, as we reached the semi-finals, before going out in that dramatic penalty shoot-out.

The next three seasons were disappointing, in that we didn't manage to build on our progress. I still got my share of goals, 27 in 1990/1991, 23 for the following season and 19 in 1992/1993.

In March 1992 I re-wrote the Wolves record books as I scored the opener in our 2-1 win at Derby. That was my 195th goal in Old Gold, passing the previous record held by the great John Richards.

At the time, records really didn't bother me. I was paid to do a job, score the goals and get us points. Records never stuck in my head and I always said at the time that I'd probably think about it more later on in life. Now I look back and think, yes, it was a big achievement. But it was an achievement that I celebrated after my retirement.

It's an honour to be up there with people like John Richards and I don't think anybody else will ever pass that record, because people these days come and go so quickly. So I'm hoping that in 50 years time, I'm still there on top of the list.

Stretching for the ball against West Brom on 5th September 1993

By that stage, Sir Jack Hayward's money was rapidly turning Molineux into one of the top grounds outside the Premier League. He's transformed it into an absolutely beautiful stadium - hardly recognisable from the ground I first played in. The only thing that's been missing is the Premiership football, but that will come in time.

Sir Jack needs a lot of credit for pumping so much money in and I just hope Wolves can repay him one day by either getting into the Premier League or winning the FA Cup.

After a third successive failure to gain promotion to the top flight, Sir Jack funded a £4 million spending spree, with Geoff Thomas, Kevin Keen, David Kelly and Peter Shirtliff coming in ahead of the 1993/1994 season.
For me it was an injury-ravaged campaign, as I missed almost 20 games with knee and ankle injuries. For Wolves it was another season of disappointment and Graham Turner paid the ultimate price - resigning in March, after seven-and-a-half years in charge.

I had a lot to thank Graham for. He gave me my big chance and had faith in my goalscoring abilities. So for me, it was like a friend going, not a manager. I was injured for his last game in charge at Portsmouth away. We lost 3-0 and Jonathan Hayward came on the coach to say the performance had been rubbish. That was the final straw for Graham Turner. He phoned me on the following day and said: "Can you come in, I'm making a decision." I asked him not to go, but he'd decided his time was up.

The man who gave me my big break was replaced by another Graham - former England boss Graham Taylor. He had an instant impact and we climbed the table, only for a return of just two points from the last three games to see us fall three points adrift of a play-off place.
Still, confidence was high going into the next season and, with Steve Froggatt, Tony Daley and Neil Emblen added to the squad, we started the season as the bookies favourites.
We ended the season with four successive draws, but still made the play-offs, booking a date with Bolton. We owed them one after losing 5-1 at Burnden Park earlier in the season. Despite that result, we really thought it was going to be our year.

We won the first-leg 2-1 at our place and only Peter Shilton kept the scoreline down. He was outstanding for them that day as we dominated the game. Bolton had always been our bogey side, but we went to Burnden Park hoping to turn them over. Sadly it was not to be and everybody connected with Wolves, the players and the fans were absolutely gutted as we lost 2-0 in the return leg.
I'd say that defeat by Bolton and the play-off defeat against Crystal Palace a couple of years later were the two low points of my time at Wolves. Nothing else even came close, because we were within sight of the Premier League, but couldn't finish the job.

"I came close to signing for Coventry City"

The Bolton defeat knocked the stuffing out of us and we started the following season poorly - winning just four of the first 16 games. That run cost Graham his job and I will always remain convinced he didn't have enough time to finish the job. He'd done brilliantly in his first season and everything was in place for him to turn it around. But Wolves were a club in a hurry and, after years of missing out, the bad start was enough to see Taylor out of a job.
On a personal level, I almost did make it into the Premier League during Taylor's time at Molineux, when I came close to signing for Coventry City.
I had four meetings with Gary Pendrey and Ron Atkinson and I couldn't make up my mind. But I woke up one morning and just thought it wasn't right for me. Apart from when I decided to call it a day, it was the hardest decision I had to make in my entire career.

Get in there!! Looking pleased with myself as I drive one in against Port Vale on 3rd September 1993, about to be mobbed by (l-r) Carl Robinson, Jamie Smith, Glen Crowe and Robbie Keane

I don't think the Wolves fans would have minded if I'd have gone to Coventry, because they knew I'd done a good job for the club. But it just wasn't right and I wanted to try and finish the job we'd started at Wolves.

Like anybody else, I could look back now and wonder what might have happened if I'd gone to Coventry, but I'm not one for regrets. If I had gone, I think I'd have had more England caps, but I'd already scored for England and gone to the World Cup, so what more did I want?

Graham Taylor was replaced by Mark McGhee and I make clear my views on Mark in another section of the book. But it has to be said that he did come close to leading us out of the First Division.

I scored a hat-trick on the opening day of his first full season in charge (1996/1997) as we won 3-1 at Grimsby and we made a great start to the campaign. At one stage we looked like the only team who might catch runaway leaders Bolton, but we won just three of the last ten games and slipped out of the automatic spots. The play-offs again beckoned.

This time we faced Crystal Palace and, after losing the first leg 3-1 at Selhurst Park, we couldn't quite turn it around at home, winning 2-1, but losing 4-3 on aggregate.

By this stage it was getting harder to shake the injuries off. Whereas earlier in my career I'd just strapped myself up and got on with it, I couldn't do that any more.

"The following season was to be my last"

The 1997/1998 season was a frustrating one for myself and the team. I struggled with far too many injuries and we could not build on the play-off defeat of the previous season. We did reach the FA Cup semi-final, but Arsenal ended any dreams of a trip to Wembley as we lost 1-0 at Villa Park.

The following season was to be my last and again I struggled with injuries. Even so, I went on our pre-season trip to Sweden in the summer of 1999 feeling fully fit and looking forward to another campaign. I didn't realise my career was about to come to a shattering end.

I trained with the other lads and in one twist and a kick, it was all over. I spoke to the physio and he said that after three operations, it was probably time to knock it on the head. That was enough for me and I knew it was the end.

I had to be honest with everybody. Giving up football was the hardest decision of my life. Perhaps if I'd carried on and dropped down the leagues, I might be in a management job now.

That's one of the few things I do regret: perhaps in the last couple of years I should have moved to a lower division side, setting my stall out in either coaching or managing. But I wanted to finish at a higher level.

So, after 306 goals in 561 games, that was the end of my playing career at Wolves. Hopefully, though, it's not the end of my Molineux story. I think the fans know that my ambition now is to return one day as manager. Hopefully I could make a success of that and I'd love to think I could finish the job we started back in 1986.

A day I'll never forget!
Beating Burnley 2-0 to win the Sherpa Van Trophy
at Wembley 29th May 1988

Chapter 5

"ALL THE BEST, BABE!"

Bully's Top Ten games

I'd hate to try and calculate just how many football matches I've played in - the figure for Wolves alone is 561 - so picking the ten which mean the most to me was a painstaking task.

As you can imagine, my favourite games are usually ones in which I've scored, although I've made an exception with a 1988 Sherpa Van Trophy final because it was such a great experience to play at Wembley.
Another of my favourite 90 minutes also took place at the famous old stadium, this time in an England shirt, and I'm sure you will understand why I've also included the international against Scotland - the day I scored on my full England debut. I went on as substitute for John Fashanu at Hampden Park, and I'll never forget his words to me as he came off and I went on: "All the best, babe!"

Of my other most memorable games, one was played in the North East, one in the North West and one at the ground where I started my professional career.
The rest took place at Molineux, although even the most ardent of Wolves followers might just be a little surprised by one of my selections...

WOLVES 4 HARTLEPOOL UNITED 1; May 9th, 1987

Wolves had already clinched a place in the first-ever play-offs when we faced Hartlepool at Molineux on the final day of the 1986-87 Fourth Division campaign.
But if the result was of little importance, our performance was sparkling and it was just a pity we couldn't reproduce it when we lost over two legs to Aldershot in the play-off final a few weeks later.

The game against Hartlepool was particularly special for me because it was the day I scored my first hat-trick for Wolves. I went on to break the club's hat-trick record, but that first one obviously holds a special place in my heart.
Not that a treble looked likely for long spells of the match. With four minutes to go, I'd scored only once, having chased a through ball and brushed aside a defender to shoot into the roof of the net after half an hour.
But I grabbed my second on 86 minutes and my third two minutes later - and the crowd went wild.
A lot of people ran on to the pitch, and some of them tried to get hold of my shirt, shorts and boots as souvenirs, but I managed to get back to the dressing room fully clothed!

WOLVES 2 BURNLEY 0; May 29th, 1988

Every footballer dreams of playing in a Wembley final, and I'm delighted to say I've done it. All right, so maybe it wasn't the FA Cup or even the League Cup, but the 1988 Sherpa Van Trophy final was certainly an occasion to savour.
A crowd of nearly 81,000 packed into the famous old stadium - more than England were getting for international matches at the time. Around 50,000 of them were Wolves supporters, and the atmosphere was electric when we walked out on to the pitch. It was so loud, you couldn't even hear what the player next to you was saying.

It was also good to hear later that supporters of both clubs had mingled in pubs and played football on the car parks without any sign of trouble.
It wasn't my first Wembley experience, because we had taken part in the FA Centenary Festival the previous month, but those games were only 20 minutes each way and the crowd was only around 25,000.
We lost 4-3 to Everton in the final of that competition, and our manager Graham Turner told us just to enjoy ourselves. But I'll never forget what he said to us afterwards: "Now you've had a taste of Wembley, let's try and get there again."

Thankfully, we did, by beating Notts County in the Sherpa Van semi-final, and that set us up for a trip back down Wembley Way. We had already won the Fourth Division championship that season, beating Burnley 3-0 both home and away, but they gave us a tougher game in the final.

On the way to my first goal in the
13th minute against Preston, November 1988

Andy Mutch put us in front with a header after I'd clipped it back to him and Robbie Dennison clinched victory with a superb second half free-kick.

I was only sorry I didn't join them on the scoresheet, because I'd scored in every other round. I had a couple of chances in the final, but it wasn't to be.
But I'm not really complaining. With Wembley now knocked down, no-one else will ever have the chance to play at the stadium as we knew it, and I count myself as very fortunate to have done that after just a couple of seasons as a professional.

WOLVES 6 PRESTON 0; November 26th, 1988
Preston's timing couldn't have been worse - from their point of view - when they came to Molineux for a Third Division match in November, 1988. A week earlier, Wolves had lost 1-0 at Grimsby in the first round of the FA Cup, and it was inevitable that someone would feel the backlash.

Poor Preston just happened to be there, but our mood was such that I reckon we would have taken apart any opposition that day. Andy Mutch and Nigel Vaughan were both on target, but the match was particularly significant for me because it was the first time I'd scored four times in a senior professional match.
I'd once hit seven for Princes End Colts, and I'd also scored five in a Wolves reserve match against Peterborough when I was on my way back after an injury. But scoring four in one game at this level was brilliant.

My first goal came in the 13th minute, a drive into the corner of the net after Sam Allardyce had failed to clear Mutch's centre, and after half an hour I collected a misplaced Preston pass and ran 40 yards or so before firing past the 'keeper as he ran out.
Just before the hour mark, Mutch won a challenge and set me up for a 10-yard drive which completed my sixth Wolves hat-trick, and I realised there was still plenty of time for me to score even more, particularly as we were so much on top. That's how it turned out. In the 76th minute, Mark Venus and Keith Downing combined for a clever one-two down the left and when the ball ran to me, I was only too happy to slot it in for my fourth goal.

WOLVES 5 PORT VALE 1; December 13th, 1988
Graham Turner always said I was never really satisfied unless I was scoring, and I suppose the inclusion of this match in my Top Ten underlines his point.
A Sherpa Van Trophy tie against Port Vale hardly seems a contender in any list of great games, and even though this was as close as we got to a derby match in those days, it attracted a crowd of under 10,000.
But to me, it was memorable because I followed up that quartet against Preston with four more goals. At the time, it seemed like I just couldn't stop hitting the net. Four days after this one, I got a hat-trick in a 6-2 thrashing of Mansfield Town.
Andy Thompson created two of my goals against Vale, providing crosses for me to score with headers in the 22nd and 74th minutes.

I was also pleased, though, with my cool 10th minute finish after Andy Mutch had flicked on a long kick from goalkeeper Mark Kendall - and even more pleased when I accepted Robbie Dennison's pass and completed my hat-trick with a delicate right-foot chip in the 66th minute.
Goals like that gave me tremendous satisfaction because a lot of people in the early days thought I relied only on pace and power to score my goals. Goals like that third one against our neighbours from the Potteries proved I was also capable of scoring goals which had a touch of finesse!

Celebrating my goal against Scotland
at Hampden Park in May 1989
With Neil Webb and Paul Gascoigne

SCOTLAND 0 ENGLAND 2; May 27th, 1989

This one just had to be included, didn't it? Even if I hadn't scored England's second goal - which I describe in detail in my Great Goals chapter - it would still have been one of the best days of my career. I enjoyed every minute of it, but it all went by so quickly and I just wish I could go back and do it all again.

The build-up to the match at Hampden Park had been special enough, and just being able to train with world class players like Paul Gascoigne, Bryan Robson and John Barnes had been incredible.

Things got even better when manager Bobby Robson named me as one of the substitutes, and as I was sitting on the bench for the first half hour, it dawned on me that I might just get on the pitch and win my first full England cap.

That, of course, is exactly what happened, and I will never forget John Fashanu's words to me when he came off injured and I replaced him. As he came over to the touchline, he said: "All the best, babe!" Nobody had ever called me that before, particularly not another bloke, but that was just Fash's way, so I shook his hand and said "Thanks."

When I went on, I felt a bit overawed by it all at first, but you just have to get the blinkers on, switch off to everything around you, and get on with your game.

Once my nerves had settled, I suddenly realised I wasn't out of place in such distinguished company. That surprised me a bit, because I was still only a Third Division player at the time.

No doubt a lot of the Scottish supporters hadn't even heard of me, but they were already a bit subdued after Chris Waddle had put us ahead in the first half - and my goal 10 minutes from time well and truly silenced the famous Hampden Roar!

NEWCASTLE UNITED 1 WOLVES 4; January 1st, 1990

Wolves fans took to the skies in their hundreds on New Year's Day, 1990, but I bet they didn't feel as high as me after I scored four second half goals.

Although the team had travelled by coach the previous day, almost every Wolves supporter who headed to Tyneside did so on specially chartered planes. Many of them were dressed as Father Christmas or wore various other fancy dress outfits, while a lot of people had gone straight to Birmingham Airport after New Year parties, and spent the night sleeping in the airport lounge. I'm told that one guy was still wearing his pyjamas under his ordinary clothes!

It certainly made for a carnival atmosphere among our supporters, although they must have wondered if the trip had been worthwhile as Wolves struggled in a goalless first half.

On one occasion, home fans at the Gallowgate End thought it was hilarious when I lost my footing and fell over in the penalty area - but they were later made to regret laughing at me!

In the second half, kicking towards the end where our fans were gathered on a small, open terrace (St James' Park was being redeveloped at the time), we really turned on the style.

Five minutes after half-time, Paul Cook took advantage of a mistake by one of Newcastle's defenders and drilled the ball low into the goalmouth. I got my foot to it at the near post and the sheer pace of the ball carried it into the bottom corner.

After another six minutes, Keith Downing played the ball through to leave me clear, and I took it round goalkeeper John Burridge before slotting it home.

I scored a similar goal later in the game, going around Burridge again after Robbie Dennison's pass had put me through, and in between times I headed in at the far post following Robbie's corner. What a way to welcome in a new decade!

On target again - this time
against Czechoslovakia

ENGLAND 4 CZECHOSLOVAKIA 2; April 25th, 1990

This was probably the match which secured my place in England's Italia '90 squad - and also the night I was really in tune with Paul Gascoigne.

For all his individual brilliance, Gazza wasn't always an easy player to anticipate, which could be frustrating both for him and the players around him. But that night at Wembley, he and I hit it off brilliantly. It occurred to me later that if we had always been like that, I would have had a sackful of goals for my country, rather than just the four I finished with.

The first, of course, had been in an unforgettable debut against Scotland 11 months earlier, and the last would come against Tunisia in a World Cup warm-up match.

But for sheer quality, those two against the Czechs were undoubtedly the best - particularly the first one.

Gazza played a superb pass with the outside of his foot and as the ball dropped over by shoulder, I chested it down and volleyed it into the roof of the net, all in one movement.

That gave me a lot of satisfaction, because it proved that players from outside London are capable of performing on the highest stage.

My second goal came when Gazza beat an opponent three or four times and then decided to cross the ball. I met it with a header into the top corner, and it was time to celebrate!

As I say, I'm sure that was the night I booked my ticket to Italy. I'd proved I was capable of scoring at international level, and I think Bobby Robson saw me as England's surprise package at the World Cup, because the other teams knew so little about me. Don't forget, I hadn't yet completed my first full season in the old Second Division, so coaches from other countries would know even less!.

WOLVES 1 MANCHESTER UNITED 2; August 3rd, 1994

Here's one which might surprise you. The game against United was only a pre-season friendly, and we were beaten into the bargain, so it hardly seems a strong contender for my Top Ten.

But that game meant everything to me. Throughout my career, people always questioned if I would have been capable of scoring in the top division, and that night I gave them the answer.

All right, so the result wasn't important, but United were a top Premiership side - they had won the title by eight points the previous season - and I took great delight in scoring with a lob over Peter Schmeichel, one of the world's top goalkeepers.

I can't remember a great deal about the rest of the match, but that single moment made it a Molineux night to treasure. These days, whenever people bring up the subject of whether I would have scored goals in the Premiership, I remind them: "Well, I did get one against Manchester United!"

I get the winner against Man City and celebrate with
Jamie Smith, Dean Richards, Neil Emblem and Mark Venus.

ALBION 2 WOLVES 4; September 15th, 1996

Iwan Roberts was the real star of this show, helping himself to a hat-trick as we trounced the old enemy in their own backyard. But the match also gave me a lot of satisfaction, and not just because we beat the Baggies.

Apart from being involved a cracking game, I had double reason to celebrate that day - a goal at the Birmingham Road End with my left foot!

The Albion fans gave me plenty of stick whenever we played them, so it was always nice to give a bit back. And what better way than by scoring right in front of them with the foot which I usually used only for standing on?

Iwan had already put us ahead when Steve Froggatt took a long throw-in from the left-hand touchline in the 15th minute. By that stage, Albion's defence were in all kinds of panic, and I was able to turn and shoot from six yards before any of them was able to react to the danger.

We'd had a flying start that season, losing only one of our first half dozen matches, and such an emphatic victory over Albion raised hopes that we were on course for promotion.

In the event, we finished third behind Bolton and Barnsley and ended up missing out to sixth placed Crystal Palace in the play-off semi-finals, which was a real blow.

But that day at The Hawthorns we were really on fire, and even though the Baggies came back at us strongly in the second half, our early onslaught meant there was never any danger of them pegging us back.

MANCHESTER CITY 0 WOLVES 1; October 27th, 1996

Maine Road was always one of my favourite grounds, and I must say I was disappointed when I heard about Manchester City's proposed move to the new Commonwealth stadium. Maybe City's long-term home had become run-down and out-dated, but for me it was a place where there was always a tremendous atmosphere - probably because Manchester City v Wolves was such a big match.

But quite apart from that, the ground was a special place for me from the first time I played there for Albion's reserves in September, 1985. I scored that night in a 1-1 draw, but what I remember most is the feel of the place, even when it was almost empty, and how far the terracing stretched back on the far side of the ground.

If anyone ever asks me about my favourite grounds, Maine Road is always one I mention, and it was extra special when we played there in front of a packed crowd in 1996.

As usual, it was a tight game, but we made the breakthrough 14 minutes from time when Denis Pearce drifted a through ball beyond their defence and I raced on to it. Kit Symons was marking me, but he got the wrong side of me and I was able to get away from him and drill a low shot into the corner of the net.

Liam and Noel Gallagher of Oasis are big City fans and they were there that day. I didn't meet them, but it gave me quite a thrill to score the winner against their team.

Maybe if people ask them to recall the game, they will say: "That bloke Bull scored the winner"!

It's the 66th minute and, although I didn't know at the time, this is my last goal for Wolves, against Bury in September 1998.

Chapter 6

GREAT GOALS
Bully's Top Ten

When I was asked to select my Top Ten favourite goals, it was no easy selection - not with more than 300 to choose from! But I sat down, went through them all and came up with the 10 which stand out most in my memory.
In some cases, they are pretty obvious; in others, Wolves fans will no doubt disagree. I reckon, in fact, that if you asked a dozen supporters to put together a list of my best goals, none of them would come up with exactly the same ones.

That's where opinion is so important, of course. Some people might recall a particular goal and wonder: "Why on earth didn't he include that one?"
But look at it from my point of view. All of my goals were special to me, so I've tended to go for the ones with extra special significance from a personal point of view as much as the actual quality of the shot or header.

I've also declined to place my Top Ten in any particular order, so they are listed in chronological order - except for number one, that is.

WOLVES 1 BURY 0; September 26th, 1998
I didn't know it at the time, but my goal against Bury was the last of my career. That makes it the most special of them all, because it's the one I signed off with.
Looking back, I'm just grateful it was at Molineux in front of the Wolves supporters who had given me such tremendous backing over the previous 12 years. I'm pleased, too, that my last senior game for Wolves was also at home, against Bradford City on the final day of that season.

To be honest, I would rate the goal against Bury as my number one even if it had been a tap-in, simply because of its significance.
As it happens, though, it wasn't a bad effort. Full-back Kevin Muscat got down the right and crossed to the far post, where I dived to head in from seven yards.
Perhaps it's as well I didn't know I would never score another goal for Wolves. If I'd known, I would have been pretty emotional.

HEREFORD UNITED 1 WOLVES 2; August 29th, 1987
If the Bury goal was the last of my career, I suppose I should also have included the first, but a lot of those early ones have faded from my memory. For the record, I scored my first Wolves goal in a Freight Rover Cup tie against Cardiff at Ninian Park a couple of weeks after signing, my first League goal was at Hartlepool, and my first Molineux goals - two of them - were in a 4-3 Freight Rover win against Bournemouth.

But the one which holds the best memories for me from that first year as a Wolves player was the one which flew into the net at Edgar Street from just outside the penalty area.
Our goalkeeper Mark Kendall threw the ball out, Nicky Clarke knocked it forward and my striking partner Andy Mutch flicked it on - he was really good at that.
I controlled it on my left thigh and although I had a defender right behind me, I just leathered it into the net! It didn't go into the top corner, but it flew above the 'keeper and I'm sure it was the sheer power of the shot which beat him.
I couldn't quite believe it, because although I'd scored more than 20 times for Wolves by then, it wasn't really my type of goal. That was a really satisfying feeling.

Proud to be playing for England.

WOLVES 1 BOLTON 0; March 4th, 1989

This was my favourite goal of the 1988-89 season. Not only did it help us on the way to promotion from the old Third Division, it was scored from 25 yards with my left foot - something I couldn't remember ever doing before.
A long ball from Andy Thompson was flicked on by Andy Mutch, I let fly - and in it went.

Until then, I'd never used my left foot unless I really had to, but our manager Graham Turner kept encouraging me to give it a go. He kept saying: "Just swing that left foot, and one of these days you'll really catch one and it will go in."
I'm delighted to say he was right, but I took him at his word after that. Every time I got the chance, I had a go with my left foot - and the ball went flying all over the place!

SCOTLAND 0 ENGLAND 2; May 27th, 1989

This is the only one of my choices which isn't a Wolves goal, but I'm sure the gold-and-black army will understand why!
To score for your country is an unforgettable experience, and to do it on your debut is almost unbelievable.
Without wishing to sound big-headed, I reckon I might have had a couple more goals that afternoon at Hampden Park if Paul Gascoigne hadn't been quite so selfish. There was one occasion when he had the ball on the byline and I was waiting in front of goal. If he'd pulled it back, I'm sure I would have scored. Instead, he tried a shot himself, but don't get the idea I'm criticising Gazza - he was a player after my own heart in that respect!

When the goal finally came, 10 minutes from time, it was an incredible feeling. Gary Stevens went down the right and put a diagonal ball towards the edge of the penalty area. I jumped up with Dave McPherson and the ball hit me on my shoulder.

My first instinct when I landed was to see where the ball was, and it was right in front of me. I struck it past Jim Leighton and into the bottom corner and it was an incredible feeling. I didn't know what to do, so I just dropped to my knees. I could have cried.

ALBION 1 WOLVES 2; October 15th, 1989

This was the first time I'd played against the Baggies since they had sold me nearly three years earlier, and I took a great deal of satisfaction from scoring our winner in the last minute at The Hawthorns.
What a superb feeling it was as Andy Mutch crossed from the right and I chested the ball down and volleyed it in one movement past Stuart Naylor at the Smethwick End.

All the Wolves fans were gathered behind that goal and they went absolutely crazy. I still love seeing them jumping up and down whenever I watch the video.
It was a different story at the Birmingham Road End, of course, and I think that was the day Albion supporters started hating me!

Over the years, a lot of Baggies fans have had a go at me about leaving them, but I've always tried to explain that it wasn't my decision.

The two all-time highest scorers in
the Black Country - Tony 'Bomber' Brown
of West Brom fame and yours truly.

DERBY COUNTY 1 WOLVES 2; March 21st, 1992

John Richards was Wolves' record scorer with 194 goals - until the 73rd minute of our match against Derby at the Baseball Ground.

John had held the record for nine years, but it goes without saying that I was delighted to relieve him of it with my 195th goal for Wolves.

The roar of our fans suggested that they were pretty happy, too, particularly as it helped us to a good away win.

I have to be honest and say it wasn't the greatest of efforts. It was described at the time as "a gentle right foot volley" but that's slightly flattering.

True, I did volley Andy Mutch's forward pass, but it was a bit lucky to go in. As I hit it, the Derby goalkeeper dived towards where it was heading - the bottom corner. But it bounced in front of him and looped over his body into the net.

That was one of the few times I ever thought about records, because everyone at Molineux had been talking about nothing else for some time. They all kept asking when I was going to reach 195 so I was fully aware what it meant when the ball went in.

I went on to reach a few other milestones over the next few years, including breaking Tony Brown's record as the all-time highest scorer in West Midlands football, but none of it ever meant quite as much as the day I became Wolves' record goalscorer.

BIRMINGHAM 1 WOLVES 1; January 6th, 1996

I was really pleased with this one because it was a long-range header and it helped us to earn a third round FA Cup replay against one of our Midland rivals.

It was a chance out of nothing, really. My striking partner Don Goodman was always willing to chase things, and he blocked a clearance by Blues' goalkeeper Kevin Poole.

The ball spun into the air and then bounced back away from goal as I was running towards the edge of the penalty area. With the ball coming towards me, I was able to use its pace to get some power behind my header, which looped over Poole and into the net.

I reckon that must be one of the longest headed goals on record, because I was around 20 yards out when I made contact. At the time, I simply acted instinctively, but if you watch it on video, you can see there was a fair bit of skill involved as well! I also scored when we beat Blues 2-1 in the replay at Molineux 11 days later.

The idea of having a message on a t-shirt under my shirt was first used to celebrate our double win over West Brom (shown here at Sheffield United) before my 300th goal at Bradford (inset) gave me another t-shirt opportunity.

NORWICH CITY 2 WOLVES 3; February 17th, 1996

I'm going to cheat a bit here by including both of my goals at Carrow Road - for a very special reason. Not only were they pretty good goals, I dedicated them both to my son, who was born on the same day.

As far as I'm concerned, it was a hat-trick, because I was also present at Joe's birth! I'd travelled with the team to East Anglia on the day before the match, but when his arrival was imminent, I travelled back through the night to be present at the big event.

Joe was born early on the Saturday morning, and then I was taken back to Norwich by taxi. That must have cost Wolves a fortune, but I should imagine they felt it was worth it as I scored twice and we beat the Canaries 3-2.

My first goal was a 25-yard chip over goalkeeper Bryan Gunn early in the match after Steve Corica had taken the ball off Ian Crook.

It was brilliant because I didn't normally score in that fashion, and as the ball went in I thought: "That one's for Joe."

Little did I realise I would be toasting his arrival in the world with a double. Towards half-time, Simon Osborn played the ball through to me and I lifted it over Gunn from six yards as the 'keeper dived.

I'm convinced that sheer adrenalin carried me through that match because I hadn't slept all night. But everything which happened that day made it worth staying awake!

WOLVES 3 BIRMINGHAM 2; March 23rd, 1996

A couple of months after my long-range header at St Andrews and my goal in the replay, I scored again against Birmingham. This time it was a league match at Molineux, but it was far more dramatic than either of those FA Cup goals. With only two or three minutes to go, it looked like Blues would take revenge for their Cup defeat because they were leading 2-1, but we staged an amazing fight back to take all three points.

Andy Thompson brought the scores level with a penalty, and just as everyone was settling for a draw, Simon Osborn played the ball through from midfield and I hit it on the run to give Wolves a memorable win.

The Birmingham fans had given me a lot of stick throughout the match, particularly when their team were in front, but that was the best possible way to answer them.

I was almost lying down when I struck the ball, and whenever I see the goal again, it makes the hairs stand up on the back of my neck.

WOLVES 2 BRADFORD CITY 1; February 19th, 1998

I hadn't played much during the winter of 1997-98, so I had a wait of nearly four months between my 299th Wolves goal and 300th. But when it finally arrived it was certainly one to savour - even if it was slightly unorthodox.

For some time, I'd been wearing a T-shirt which read: "This is my 300th goal, have a good year!" and it finally happened in that match.

I was on the bench against Bradford, but when I went on I had the satisfaction of not only reaching a milestone but scoring a last-minute winner.

Lee Naylor made a great run down the left and I was beyond the far post. When he crossed superbly behind Bradford's back four, I dived in and the ball hit me on the ear!

Their 'keeper was following the flight of the ball, but it went back across him and into the net. Maybe I was a bit lucky with that one, but I wasn't complaining!

Chapter 7
THE MANAGERS

Graham Turner

Looking back at the managers I've played under, Graham Turner has to come in at number one. That's not just because he was my first manager at Wolves, but because he was such a big influence. He was the man who give me my first real chance.

Some managers are master-tacticians, some are motivators and in Graham's case, his biggest strength was without doubt his man-management. It seems like common sense to say that a football manager should know how to manage players, but I was to see later in my Wolves career that that's not always the case.
Graham, though, perfected the art and that really made you want to play for him. He knew when to pick the team up and when to give them a boot up the backside and he very rarely, if at all, got that wrong.

If you're going to succeed in management, you won't do it by being fierce all the time. At the same time, you won't do it by being one of the lads and a bit of a soft touch. But if you manage to walk a fine line between the two, you stand a chance of doing well.
I knew I was on a winner from the minute he signed me. I'd made the short journey from Albion to Wolves and he just said to me: "I've brought you here to score goals, so just get out there and do your job."
That was music to my ears as a striker, because I always say you're either a finisher or you're not. I knew I could score goals and here was a bloke who was willing to give me the chance. I wasn't going to let him down.

Of course he did have an influence on my game. I knew I wasn't the finished article when I joined Wolves and the main thing Graham worked on was my first touch. But he didn't try to coach my natural game out of me and I'll always be grateful to him for that.
It was always the same, before games. He did look at the other team, but he always told us to concentrate on our own strengths.

That was Graham all over. He knew how to get the best out of the lads. If we wanted to improve parts of our game, he told us: "My office door is always open." But he didn't try to turn you into something you weren't. Because of that, he was always one of those managers you wanted to do well for.

Graham did a terrific job for Wolves, steering the club from the old Fourth Division up to what's now the First Division, but I think his finest moment came with the Sherpa Van Final in 1988.

It might not be the most important competition in the world to some people, but our preparation for that Wembley game with Burnley couldn't have been more professional if we'd been building up to an FA Cup Final.
Graham's planning was absolutely spot-on. He got everything right from pre-match meals, to training sessions - everything went like clockwork and we got the result.

That's not to say it was all work and no play that week. We went out to Spain as part of the preparations and he came out one morning wearing dark glasses. He said it was hay fever, but we knew it was a bit too much red wine the night before!
If I had to sum Graham up, I'd have to admit he can be a bit of a dour individual, though not all the time. I've also seen the other side to him, when he's had a few beers inside him. He likes a laugh like the rest of us, but he has a real desire to win games and he knows how to get the best out of players to make sure he gets those results.

Graham Taylor

When Graham Turner was sacked in November 1994 he was replaced by another Graham - Taylor. And I will always be convinced that the former England boss would have steered Wolves into the Premier League, if only he'd been given a bit longer in the job.

Everything was spot-on with Graham and the first thing that struck me with him was his attention to detail.
Big things were expected of him when he took on the task of bringing top-flight football back to Molineux. He'd been England manager, where it hadn't quite worked out, but his track record in club management was very impressive. Because of that, the lads instantly had a lot of respect for him.

Once we spoke to him and got to know his ways and his views on the game, we really felt he could do the job and take us up.
He didn't manage to do that of course, but I actually think deep down that if he'd stayed on, he would have taken Wolves into the Premiership. He got us into the play-offs in 1995 and if he'd stayed for just another year, he would have finished the job.

He'd built on what Graham Turner had left and I don't think he was a million miles away from completing the job. I don't know whether other people at the club now have regrets about that, but I'll always regret that he didn't get the chance to complete the job.
The turning point for Graham was the play-off defeat against Bolton. We should have won both of those games, but it just wasn't our year and we were absolutely sick to miss out. I think it really did for Graham and he wasn't at the club for much longer.
As I say, that was a real shame. Who knows what he might have gone on to achieve if he'd stayed?

Mark McGhee

If Graham Taylor was unlucky, then his successor Mark McGhee simply got it wrong and blew the chance of finishing the job.
He was seen as a rising star of management when he walked out on Leicester and took over at Wolves in December 1995. Obviously he played under Alex Ferguson at Aberdeen and the papers were calling him 'The new Fergie'. He didn't really live up to that billing.
Everything was in place for Mark when he came to Wolves. We hadn't started the season well, but this was a side that had reached the play-offs in the previous season and we were good enough to go one better.
After a tricky first season, Mark did get us into the play-offs the following season. But after we lost again - this time to Crystal Palace - I think a lot of players lost faith and a bit of respect for him.
We'd built up a great team spirit as we'd climbed from the old Fourth Division, but that was lost a bit during Mark's time at Wolves.

I think money played a big part. I always say money will spoil anybody and when we got the big-money signings coming in, they were suddenly the stars of the team and it spoiled the spirit.
It was always my dream to play for Wolves in the Premiership and although I wouldn't exactly blame Mark for the fact that I never fulfilled that dream, he did get things wrong.

I don't think you can ever blame the manager - the players are the ones who win or lose games. But the players actually lost faith in Mark and that was hard to turn around.
If my first Wolves boss Graham Turner was the sort of manager you'd walk through walls for, that wasn't the case with Mark McGhee. As I say, we're not all naturals when it comes to man-management.

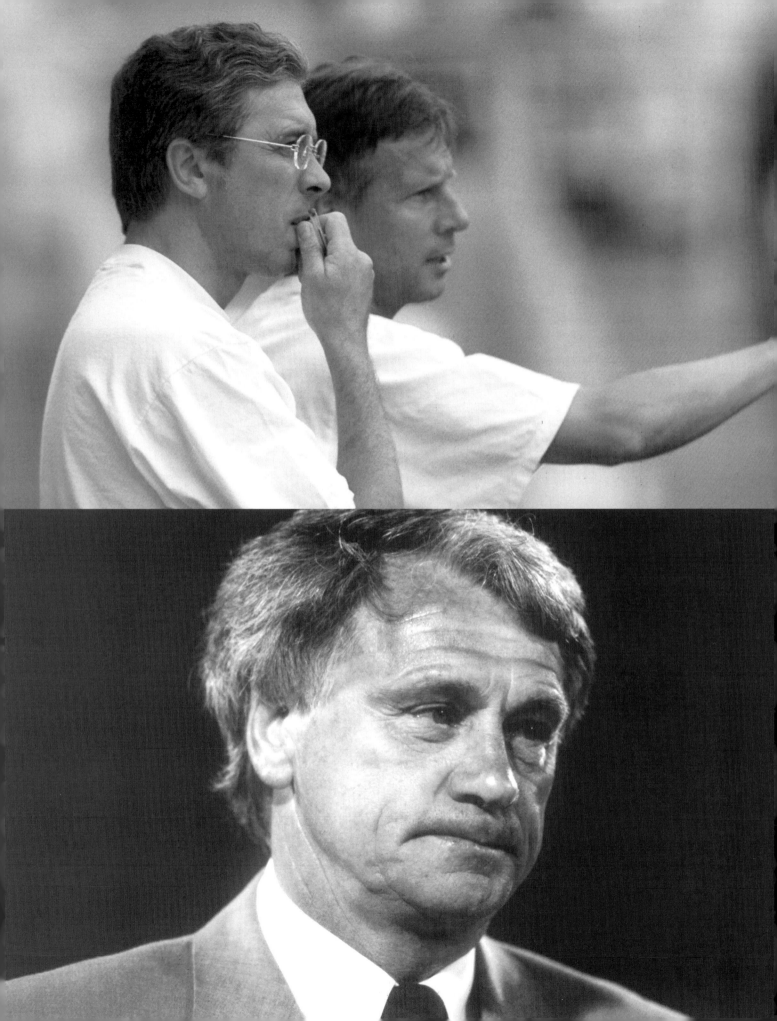

Colin Lee

Just like in any walk of life, the different managers I had in my time at Wolves had different strengths. Colin Lee would have to go down as the master-tactician. Colin lives and breathes football and he plans things down to the very last detail. He's so thorough and he knows all about the opposition, but he will listen to your opinion as well and I think that's important.

I know Colin comes across as a quiet, unassuming bloke, but that's not the case in the dressing room. If he has something to say or he thinks you've done something wrong, he'll let you know about it. But he's always constructive.

It came as a surprise when Colin took over from Mark McGhee, because, more often than not, when a manager goes he takes his backroom staff with him.
But Colin came in and told the lads: "The club have asked me to take over for however long it takes to find a new manager, so carry on doing what you're doing and I'll try to get the best out of you."

It was possibly a gamble, because Mark McGhee had lost the respect of the lads, but Colin made sure it was like a fresh start and he got the best out of the team.
Obviously I didn't get to play under Colin for too long and I often wonder if he might have helped me improve my game. I tried to take something from all my gaffers at Wolves and maybe Colin's attention to detail could have taught me a few things.

Bobby Robson

If I'm talking about the managers I played under, I have to mention Sir Bobby Robson - after all this is the man who took me to the World Cup and that's something nobody can ever take away from me.
It's difficult to think that what would now be a Second Division player might get into the current England squad, but Sir Bobby had the courage of his convictions when he called me up. He felt I could do a job and I was determined not to let him down.

We were in the Third Division and I was a bit of an unknown quantity at the time. So when he selected me for the Scotland game he just told me: "Nobody knows anything about you, so just go out there and do what you've been doing for Wolves. Just do your job."

I've always felt that you should pick the man in form and that's exactly what he did. At that time I was scoring goals and that was good enough for Sir Bobby.
Some players just go along for the ride with England, but I knew I could do a job for him and I knew that if he picked me, I wouldn't let him down.

Bobby Robson is a man who commands respect from his players and part of his success is that he shows his players respect. Now I don't care what walk of life you're in, if you treat people right, they'll do a job for you.
His enthusiasm rubs off on everybody. He's never lost that love of the game that you have as a kid and he's as desperate to be a winner now as he ever was.

That will to win almost won the ultimate prize for England in 1990. I think it was the best chance we've had to lift the World Cup since 1966 and we just fell at that last hurdle. It wasn't down to Sir Bobby that we failed to go all the way, that's just how it goes in cup football. You need the breaks if you're going to win a tournament and we didn't really get them in that semi-final against Germany.

Chapter 8

GREAT PLAYERS OF MY ERA

Andy Mutch

As I look back at all my team-mates down the years, the first man I have to mention is Andy Mutch - my partner in crime as I made a name for myself at Molineux. Between us we scored the goals that got Wolves from the old Fourth Division to what is now the First Division.

I think when Graham Turner brought us together in 1986, the Wolves fans were looking for heroes and, as is often the case, they latched onto the two goalscorers.

We just clicked straight away and it was just one of those matches made in heaven. Mutchy knew where I was, I knew where he was and whether it was in the channels, over the top or to feet, we just knew. It was definitely an instinct thing, because him being a Scouser and me being a Black Country lad, we never really had a clue what we were saying to each other. Fortunately we let our football do the talking.

"I wouldn't have done so well without Mutchy being there"

We had seven years together where I scored 217 goals and he got 105. In this day and age, with the crosses that are going in now, we'd have probably doubled the amount of goals between us.

Obviously he wasn't as prolific as I was, but I don't think he got the recognition he deserved for his work-rate and his contribution to what we did.

I know people possibly look back now and say: "Well it was Bully scoring all the goals." But I know I wouldn't have done so well without Mutchy being there.

That said, I think he was perhaps too unselfish in the box. I always wanted to see him go for goal more, but that was his game. I didn't have the same first touch and I couldn't hold the ball up as well as Mutchy, but I compensated with goals. So I suppose that's what helped make it such a good combination.

Andy Thompson

I made the short journey from West Brom to Wolves on the same day as Andy Thompson and we were firm friends from day one.

It was a good thing having a familiar face, because it can be strange walking into a new dressing room. You can fall victim to all sorts of practical jokes, but I think it was a case of strength in numbers and we got away with it.

Tommo was a definite 100 per cent player who would always work hard and do everything asked of him. You could play him in any position and you knew he'd go out and do a job for you. He even played up front with me a couple of times, but mostly he left the scoring to the experts.

He was one of the smallest blokes around with one of the biggest gobs. He shouted for fun in training and in matches and he was always having a laugh. You need that in the dressing room.

I roomed with Tommo for seven years and I'll never forget a time when I was on the receiving end of one of his practical jokes. We travelled to Norwich in February 1996 and my ex-wife was about to give birth to our second child. Tommo got into the room before me, jumped on the bed and one of the legs broke. So he put his stuff on the other bed and left the dodgy one to me. I sat down on the broken one, went arse over tit and found he'd propped it up on two bricks.

As it happened, I had to go back in the middle of the night, because my ex-wife's waters broke. So I had to travel back home and then I came back to score two goals in a 3-2 win.

Steve Froggatt

At any football club you have your fair share of snappy dressers, the blokes who always seem to have the latest style and look good. Froggy wasn't one of them.

Instead he was one of those blokes who looked scruffy no matter what he wore. He'll kill me for saying this, but he could spend a grand on a suit and still look like he'd nicked it.

One time he came in wearing a cream suit and he thought he looked the dogs bollocks, but then some of the lads went to Vegas and saw a poster of Forest Gump with the same suit on. So you can guess what his nickname was after that.

If his dress sense left a lot to be desired, there was nothing wrong with Froggy's football. He really could run for fun. He could get up and down that wing all day without getting tired. Add to that the fact that he was a great crosser of a ball and it was a great combination.

Unfortunately Steve suffered with so many injuries, which was a tragedy. That cost him an England place and ultimately brought his career to a premature close.

It was a real shame, because, bearing in mind all the problems England have had on the left down the years, I really think Froggy could have been the man to fill the gap.

He was as fit as a butcher's dog and I certainly appreciated the service from the left during his time at Wolves. He was at Molineux from 1994 to 1998 and, when fit, he was a great player.

Robbie Keane

One man I'd like to have played with earlier in my career was Republic of Ireland international Robbie Keane. We had just two seasons together and because I had my injury problems, we didn't play alongside each other as often as I would have liked.

To me Robbie was a frustrating player. Very skilful, but very frustrating. He's one of those very tricky players who can try ten things and when one of them comes off it looks great.

That's not having a go, because he wouldn't be the special player that he is without that unpredictability. But there were times when I just wanted him to do the simple things.

I wouldn't say Robbie's a natural goalscorer, but he does know where the goal is. A natural scorer will just get his head down and shoot, where Robbie prefers to trick his way past a couple of players and then put the ball in the net. The thing is, he has the ability to do that and crowds love it.

In a way he compares to Gazza, because he loves to entertain and when we played together at Wolves, he was always trying tricks out, staying behind after training to perfect something new. Sometimes that worked in matches, sometimes it didn't.

We all knew from day one at Wolves that we had a special talent in Robbie. Even then, at such a young age, he was a cocky little bugger, but a skilful player.

I still speak to him and he's had some big money moves since leaving Wolves, but it hasn't gone to his head. He's still a down-to-earth lad. He saves his cockiness for the pitch.

Mike Stowell

Mike Stowell took over from Mark Kendall in the Wolves goal and we had about seven or eight years together.
He was well liked on the terraces and I think if you ask Wolves fans who was the best keeper in my time at the club, most of them will say Mike Stowell without any hesitation.
He's a big lad, standing 6ft 2ins, so he never worried about coming for crosses; even in training. He was also a good shot stopper, so that's not a bad combination.
I think most players have a bit of a sense of humour, it keeps you sane when things are going wrong. But keepers are a breed on their own and Stowelly was no exception. He was bubbly all the time and if there was any chance to wind the lads up, cutting socks up and hiding clothes and stuff, he took it. You need that in the dressing room.

"Mike was the man
to do a job at the back"

He played over 400 games for Wolves and was a great servant to the club. I always felt confident knowing he was in goal for us.
When you play that many games for a club, it's hard to pick out just one. But one of the games that sticks in my mind came towards the end of the 1996 season. We weren't going too well and we travelled up to Oldham desperate for points. Mike had been under a bit of pressure, but he saved a Gerry Creaney penalty to earn us a point and I don't think he ever really looked back. Every player, in whatever position, goes through the bad spells, but Mike had the character to ignore the critics and bounce back.
Like all good keepers, Mike's game wasn't just about his technical abilities. He also had a big mouth and certainly let you know he was there. He ranted and raved for fun and made sure he kept his defenders on their toes. He probably used to annoy the defenders at times, but it was his box and you either did things right or he told you about it. I always knew I could do my job at the one end and Mike was the man to do a job at the back. He stopped them, I scored them and we were both happy.

Steve Walsh

When I came up against Steve Walsh at Leicester, it was always a showdown that the press, the fans and everyone looked forward to. It was a case of "Go and get the boxing gloves on again."
We were very similar characters on the pitch. If that ball was there and somebody was in my way, I'd knock him out of the way to get it. Steve was just the same, so when we came head-to-head you could always guarantee fireworks.
I always loved that sort of contest and I knew that off the field Steve was sound as a pound. We're not the best of mates or anything like that, but there was a mutual respect. We both wanted to do it for the team and nothing got in the way. You can't teach somebody to have that streak of determination.

We're only talking about the nineties, but I don't think Steve could really get away with that sort of no-nonsense defending now. I had defenders coming through the back of me, elbowing, head-butting, the lot. I'm not saying Steve did all of those every time I came up against him, but I always knew I'd been in a game when we played Leicester. He wasn't a head-case, just a hard player.

Even while we were taking lumps out of each other, I always thought he was the sort of player we missed at Wolves. He was a leader and he took Leicester to a few promotions, while we just couldn't get into the Premier League. Perhaps if we'd had a Steve Walsh, it might have been different.

Dean Richards

Deano was a top, top player and I could never understand why Wolves let him go. But Southampton paid the asking price and off he went. He's since gone on to be a top Premier League defender.

He was brought to the club by Graham Taylor in the summer of 1995 and was a bit raw when he first came to the club. But Graham saw something in the young lad from Bradford and he was spot-on.

It wasn't as if Deano could grow in size, because he was a massive bugger when he came to Wolves, but he certainly grew in stature.

He certainly wasn't a Steve Walsh type defender. He was more of a ball-player and you could see the touches in his game from the first day. But he was raw, a bit like me when I first joined. What he's achieved since leaving Wolves is down to dedication and sheer hard work.

Coming from Bradford with that thick Yorkshire accent, nobody could understand him, so he was a quiet lad in the Molineux dressing-room.

He was a quiet lad on the field as well, but I think he's developed that side of his game now. He realises he's good enough and he roasts his players.

Deano was another one of those players at Wolves who would have done a job for us in the Premier League, but it wasn't to be.

Paul Cook

If Gazza was the man to create the openings for me at England level, Paul Cook did the job at Wolves.

Cookie had the sweetest left foot you could wish for and he could put the ball wherever I wanted it, whenever I wanted it. It was a bit like the partnership with Andy Mutch, in that Cookie knew exactly where I'd want the ball. He didn't even need to look up half the time.

"Cookie had the sweetest left foot you could wish for"

We clicked instantly and he helped me score a lot of goals during his five years at Molineux. Perhaps he could have scored a few more himself, but he was the playmaker.

He was a typical cocky Liverpudlian. He and Mutchy would travel in together and it was like the Scouse mafia in the dressing-room. The one blessing was that, being a Tipton lad, I couldn't understand a word they were saying. But we certainly understood each other on the pitch.

Some flair players can often be accused of not pulling their weight, but Cookie was one of the fittest players I ever played with and that explains why he was still playing well into his thirties.

Paul Gascoigne

At the time I broke into the England side Paul Gascoigne was clicking with Peter Beardsley and Gary Lineker and that was a hard threesome to break up.

But when I did get my chance to team up with Gazza, I thought: "He can do a job for me." It was like Paul Cook and Simon Osborn at Wolves. They could find me anywhere on the pitch and Gazza was the same on the international stage.

Some players are good characters in the dressing room, but Gazza was something else. He's round the bend and there was never a dull moment. Luckily, he never stitched me up, but he'd have the lads in fits.

Gazza at his best was always trying tricks during matches, but if they didn't come off, he had the work-rate to tackle back and have another go.

"There was never a dull moment with Gazza"

He was one of those players who, even when he became a professional, and a bloody good one at that, still played like he did as a kid. He was always the same. Even in training, he'd try and nutmeg you and leave you on your backside. But I saw after just one training session with England just how talented he was.

A lot of people use that label 'world-class', but you don't get to play with too many genuine world-class players. Gazza was one man who deserved the title.

He had almost everything. He could do things with the ball that you'd never dream of and that's what people want to see. If he'd had my knack of scoring goals, he'd have been the complete player.

Chapter 9

THAT MAN RUSH
A few thoughts on my idol

Wolves will always be the team nearest to my heart after all my years at Molineux, but I'm actually a Liverpool supporter! I've only recently managed to get to see the Reds at Anfield, but from as far back as I can remember, they have been my favourite team.

I suppose my love for Liverpool goes back to when I was growing up in Tipton. I never went to matches in the Midlands because I was usually playing for local sides on Saturday afternoons, but I became a keen armchair follower of the Merseysiders when they were so successful in the late seventies and early eighties.
They seemed to be on television all the time in those days, when they kept winning the European Cup, and I suppose that's what attracted me, in the same way that a lot of youngsters in the Black Country now follow clubs like Manchester United and Arsenal.

"When Ian Rush came on the scene
I found myself a role model"

The first Liverpool players who caught my attention were Kevin Keegan and Kenny Dalglish, but it was when Ian Rush came on the scene that I found myself a role model. Even in such a great team, he somehow stood out from the rest.

There's no doubt about it, Rushie was a great finisher, and the thing which stuck in my mind most about him was how selfish he was in the penalty area.
Whenever he got the ball in the box, he always wanted to shoot, rather than pass to a team-mate, and it's fair to say I was very much the same sort of player. Maybe I never played at the same level as him, but I don't think anyone can argue with our respective goalscoring records!

My one disappointment was that I never had the chance to see Ian play live, nor play against him. But I came mighty close to playing alongside him on one occasion. When the English League played the Italian League in a representative match in Naples in January, 1991, we were both in the squad - and I actually went on to replace Rush. Unfortunately, neither of us lived up to our goalscoring reputations that day. The Italians beat us 3-0.

I didn't say a great deal to Ian on that trip. Even though I'd played in the World Cup by then, I suppose I was still a bit overawed at meeting my childhood hero. But he had plenty to say to me the next time we met.
That was after I'd retired, and I'd started working towards my UEFA "A" coaching badge. I had to go to Wales for part of the course and he was one of the instructors.
At one point, he organised a session for forwards, outlining what was needed both for strikers as individuals and players who operate as pairs.

As a former player, I was an obvious choice to demonstrate the points he was trying to get across to other people on the course because some of them were from other walks of life and hadn't played football.
Obviously, he had to tell me what I should be doing, but I kept thinking: "Hold on, I did this for 16 years!"
But I didn't say anything. Throughout my career, I'd always listened to what my managers and coaches had to say, and tried to follow their instructions. It didn't seem right to start arguing with a coach who was trying to teach people about the game - particularly when it was the guy I'd idolised as kid.

Representing England under 21's against Albania under 21's, March 1989

Chapter 10

BACKSTREET INTERNATIONAL
Playing for England

If I thought my first taste of international football would be a refreshing change from the physical nature of life in the lower divisions, I couldn't have been more wrong.

The setting was certainly different to anything I'd ever experienced because we were playing in poverty-stricken Albania, and we even took our own chef - a guy called Roger Narbett from Birmingham - because the local diet was dodgy, to say the least. But our opponents' defenders that Tuesday night in March, 1989, were as tough and uncompromising as anything I'd come across at Hartlepool, Rochdale or Aldershot.

All the same, it was a major step for me. Dave Sexton, the England Under-21 manager, had said a few months earlier that he was monitoring my progress, and he was as good as his word when he called me up as an over-age player for that game against Albania's youngsters. Despite the battering I received that afternoon, I got the feeling that my game could only improve by playing alongside international players.

Six weeks later I was able to prove the point. The attendance at Ipswich for the return match against Albania was only just over 6,000 but the crowd that night included four coach-loads of Wolves fans - and I was delighted to reward their long trek to East Anglia with my first international goal.

Steve Sedgley played the ball over the top of the defence and I chested it down and hit it with my right foot. It went under the 'keeper's body and the Wolves fans behind the goal went mad. It was great to score for them.

Myself and my Molineux striking partner Andy Mutch were then picked for the end-of-season England B tour. England opened with a 2-0 win over Switzerland and then I scored our second goal as we beat Iceland by the same score in Reykjavik - although my memories of that match are more of the weather.

Only 750 people turned up, and they must have wondered why they had bothered. It was raining heavily, and I've never played in such freezing conditions. At half-time we couldn't even hold our cups of tea because our hands were so cold. We had to go in the showers to thaw them out. My arms went pink, and Andy Mutch took over from Paul Stewart early in the second half because Paul just couldn't stop shivering.

If I was freezing cold that day, though, I was feeling increasingly comfortable about playing for my country.

In the final game against Norway in Stavanger, we were awarded a penalty after about an hour, when one of their defenders handled on the line, but no-one seemed to want to take the kick.

Dave Sexton hadn't said who should take a penalty if we got one, so I just picked the ball up and put it on the spot. I knew the 'keeper was likely to dive one way or the other, so I blasted it straight down the middle and into the roof of the net. I probably surprised even myself with that one. After all, I wasn't even Wolves' recognised penalty taker - that was Andy Thompson's job - but there's no doubt I was growing in confidence.

It was probably just as well, bearing in mind the surprise which awaited me after I got back home. I kept a low profile the day after my return, deliberately avoiding any telephone calls because I knew the Press would be chasing me to talk about my goals against Iceland and Norway. What I didn't realise was that Wolves secretary Keith Pearson was also trying to track me down to give me some important news.

When he finally contacted me, he asked which I wanted first - the bad news or the good. I opted for the bad, and it was that I had to pack my suitcase again, less than 24 hours after returning from the B tour. The good news, though, was that I was in the full England squad for the big match against Scotland at Hampden Park that weekend. I felt shattered, but I wasn't about to turn down a chance like that!

The next few hours were a bit of a blur. After chatting with Keith, I managed to get on a flight to Glasgow, where I was met by a chauffeur-driven Jaguar and taken to England's hotel at Troon. It was after 11pm by the time I met manager Bobby Robson and checked in, and I was feeling pretty hungry by then so I ordered some chicken sandwiches and two pints of milk before heading off to my room.

Closely marked by Yugoslavia's Predrag Spasic

Over the next couple of days, I trained with some of the country's most famous footballers, people like Peter Shilton, John Barnes and Bryan Robson and I was absolutely delighted when the squad was named on the Friday morning and I was included in the five substitutes.

I was aware, too, that John Fashanu had injured his knee in a match against Chile at Wembley earlier that week, and that although he was in the starting line-up alongside Tony Cottee, there was every chance he wouldn't last the full 90 minutes.

Bobby Robson knew as much, too. On the day of the match, we left the hotel for Hampden Park at around 1pm and I found myself sitting by myself on the coach, probably because I just didn't know the other players well enough. But Bobby came and sat by me, and said he would have no worries about putting me on if he had to. That's when it started to dawn on me that I might well be involved in the action, and when Fash was forced to come off after only half an hour, Bobby Robson's assistant Don Howe told me I was to replace him. Don's orders were brief and to the point - I was just to play my normal game and not try anything clever.

"Nothing can take away the memories of playing for my country"

That's exactly what I did, and it didn't work out too badly. I've talked more about the game and my goal in England's 2-0 win elsewhere in this book, and it goes without saying that day in Glasgow was one I'll never forget.

The night we beat Czechoslovakia 4-2 at Wembley the following April was also a great occasion. I'd gained further international experience by then, playing against Denmark in Copenhagen and Yugoslavia at Wembley, but I'm convinced it was my performance and two goals against the Czechs which clinched my place in the 1990 World Cup squad.

My other England goal came in a World Cup warm-up match in Tunisia, and I really enjoyed my time in Italy that summer, particularly as I played at least some part in the group matches against Ireland, Holland and Egypt, as well as the second-round victory over Belgium.

Unfortunately, my international career was over by October that year. Graham Taylor had taken over as manager from Bobby Robson after the World Cup, and although I was involved in the Wembley victories over Hungary and Poland, the 2-0 win over the Poles was the last time I pulled on the white shirt of England.

I was bitterly disappointed not to be given another chance, but nothing can take away the memories of playing for my country.

Seen here in action against Belgium
on 26 June during England's
1990 World Cup campaign

Chapter 11

THE WORLD AT MY FEET
Italia '90

You can't get a full English breakfast in Italy, but I wouldn't have missed the 1990 World Cup finals for anything. I'd already played for the full England team by then, and scoring on my debut against Scotland will obviously always be special to me.
But being involved for my country in football's most prestigious tournament was an incredible experience, even if it meant having to manage without bacon and eggs for six weeks!

It was a long time to be away, much longer than anything I'd known before, and I have to admit there were times when I became homesick. But while I missed my cooked breakfast, the rest of the food was fine, even for a Black Country lad like me. Whatever you wanted, the chefs cooked for you - except bacon and eggs for breakfast! And what an opportunity it was to be part of Bobby Robson's squad as they chased glory at Italia '90. I'd certainly like to turn the clock back and do it all over again.

In the end, of course, it all ended in tears - particularly for Paul Gascoigne - when we lost in a penalty shoot-out to Germany in the semi-finals. It was a great pity, because that squad should have won the World Cup. It was the best side I've known and I still can't quite believe we didn't win it, rather than having to settle for fourth place after we lost to Italy, the other beaten semi-finalists, in the play-off match.

"Keep yourself fit, keep out of trouble, and you'll be all right"

With the obvious exception of 1966, that was the best England squad in my lifetime. Apart from Gazza, you had the likes of Peter Shilton, Gary Lineker, Peter Beardsley and David Platt, all of them world-class players. Just to be with them for such a big event was an incredible feeling, because I'd only had one season as a Second Division footballer at the time and they were big names around the globe. Platty, in fact, was my room-mate while we were out there, and apart from being a great player, he was also good company.

I knew I was in line for a seat on the plane to Italy when Graham Turner had a word with me at the end of that season. Managers always know first if their players are about to get an international call-up, and Graham told me: "Keep yourself fit, keep out of trouble, and you'll be all right."
About a week later, I received the letter which told me I was in Bobby Robson's squad, and I'm convinced to this day that it was my performance and two goals in the 4-2 win over Czechoslovakia a few weeks earlier which clinched my selection.

My chance of actually playing some part in the finals was also helped when I scored in a 1-1 draw against Tunisia in a warm-up game before we settled at our base in Cagliari for the group matches.
With so many talented players in the squad, I was never sure whether or not I would get a game, but to be honest, I was just happy to be there. As it turned out, I got involved right from the start. I went on as substitute for Lineker in the opening game, a 1-1 draw against the Republic of Ireland, and then replaced Chris Waddle in the goalless draw with Holland before making the starting line-up against Egypt.

That wasn't one of my better games for England, but the important thing was that we won 1-0 and clinched a place in the second round. The match in Bologna will always be remembered for Platty's spectacular over-the-shoulder volley in the last minute of extra-time, but I often think it could have been my moment of glory.

Just a few of the many Good Luck cards
I was sent during the Italia '90 campaign

I'd replaced John Barnes towards the end of normal time, and when that late free-kick drifted into the penalty area, I was standing right behind Platt. I often think about what I might have happened if he hadn't made contact, because I was in a perfect position to score. That would certainly have been one for my club manager Graham Turner to savour because he was in the stadium that night, along with quite a few Wolves fans. Not that I'm complaining. It was a brilliant goal, and I was the first player to reach Platty and celebrate our last-gasp victory.

Unfortunately, that was my last action in Italy. I was on the bench for the quarter-final win against Cameroon and the semi-final against the Germans, although at one stage I thought I might get on in that game. Bobby Robson had told me to get ready, but then Lineker scored and the boss told me to put my tracksuit top back on!

"Being involved in football's most prestigious tournament was an incredible experience"

It was a disappointment, not only for me but for hundreds of Wolves fans who had sent me 'Good Luck' messages via the Express & Star's man in Italy, Martin Swain.
Rather than give me all the letters together, Martin used to bring some each day to our training headquarters, and I have to say they made me feel at home.

Many of them contained pictures of me, drawn by schoolchildren and and I also had letters signed by entire classes from schools in the West Midlands. After a while it all became a bit embarrassing because the other players kept taking the mickey about my fan mail, but I really appreciated those letters from home. I tried to respond to as many as possible when I got home, but it was just impossible. So if you sent me a letter, thanks. And if you didn't get a reply, sorry!

While I thoroughly enjoyed Italia '90, though, I don't think I could have coped with playing abroad on a permanent basis. I've always been a homely person, and six weeks is long enough to go without a cooked breakfast!

Chapter 12

WOLF CUBS

When I'm asked about the next generation of stars at Wolves, three players really stand out for me. It's not that I don't rate the other young lads at Molineux, but it is hard to know with some of them, because so many promising youngsters tend to fall by the wayside. I could give a long list of kids who certainly have plenty of ability, but they have to overcome a lot of obstacles to really make the grade.

Keith Andrews

Sometimes it can be hard to put your finger on it, but you just know that a young lad is going to make the grade and be a good player. That's been my view of Keith Andrews since I first saw him play for Wolves reserves in the late nineties.

In my opinion the young Irish midfielder is a leader. He has an old head on his shoulders and he's the sort of player you want when the tackles start flying in the middle of the park. He reminds me a bit of Jamie Pollock when he first started out at Middlesbrough.

Keith hasn't really grabbed the headlines like some of the youngsters down the years at Wolves, but I'm convinced he has what it takes to be a top-class midfielder. He gets stuck in, but he can play a bit as well. For every flair player, you need somebody like Keith and though fans don't always appreciate that,   managers do.

Matt Murray

As with all goalkeepers, it will be years before Matt Murray reaches his peak. But he's definitely a promising young talent who looks like he has what it takes to become a star.

He had his share of injuries as a young lad and must have wondered whether he would make the grade. But he has battled through the problems and now looks ready to live up to his potential.

Matt certainly has the build to be a quality 'keeper, but he's agile for a big lad. He's a good shot stopper and I can see why big things are expected from him.

Like Joleon Lescott, he's already played for England Under-21s and that must mean he's heading in the right direction.

Matt has all the basic attributes needed to be a good 'keeper; the presence that the top 'keepers have will only come with experience. So he has to keep working hard.

Joleon Lescott

One youngster I have no doubt about is Joleon Lescott. The kid is quality and I have no hesitation in saying that he will play for the full England side one day.

Joleon has everything you want in a central defender. He's a big lad, he's quick, good in the air and he has a good first touch. Put all those qualities together and you know you're on to a winner.

He made his debut for Wolves in 2000 and he hasn't really looked back since. He's won the Young Player of the Year Award a couple of times and he's getting better all the time. Playing for a First Division side means he already has over 100 first-team appearances to his name, which might not have been the case with a Premier League side. That experience will hold him in good stead.

Joleon has already played for England at youth level and for the Under-21s, so I'm sure a lot of people in the Premier League are aware of his ability.
If Wolves can reach the top flight, this is one player who can certainly make the step up. No doubt about it.

I really feel that Joleon, Matt and Keith are going places. But the three of them will be aware that they have to keep working hard and improving their game. You can have all the natural ability in the world, but what makes top players is that they also graft hard and they have the desire to do well.

Chapter 13
TODAY'S GREAT STRIKERS

Alan Shearer

When I look at the great strikers currently doing the business in the Premiership, I have to say that the first man I look at is Alan Shearer. For me he's one of a dying breed - the bustling forward who puts his head in where it hurts. His record speaks for itself and the fact that he keeps banging the goals in, season after season, shows that he's still hungry for more.

He's scored a century of goals for two clubs in the Premier League and that's even allowing for a few lengthy lay-offs with injury. It's an amazing achievement.

If I have one criticism of Alan, it's that I think he retired from international football too soon. I watched the World Cup in Japan and thought he was the missing link. He could have done a job for Sven Goran Eriksson, leading the younger lads. Obviously that was his decision, but I think he got it wrong.

That said, nobody at Newcastle is complaining and Sir Bobby Robson is now getting even more from Alan. He leads by example at St James Park and, playing for his hometown club, it's no wonder he's such a big hero.

Ruud Van Nistelrooy

Another striker who grabs plenty of headlines is Ruud Van Nistelrooy and I have to say that he's got the one thing all great strikers must have - he's selfish.
He only has one thing on his mind when he gets the ball anywhere near goal and that's why he gets so many goals. It's no good constantly looking around for your team-mates, you have to have confidence in your ability and go for it.

Van Nistelrooy can be physical and he shows touches of skill, but really his game is about one thing. That's scoring goals and he doesn't mind how they come. Some players just score spectacular goals, but goalscorers get their share of the ugly ones as well.

He's scored plenty for United, but I have to say that any striker worth his salt would fancy his chances at Old Trafford, because the players around you will always create chances. That's why it always amazed me that the goals dried up for Andy Cole and Dwight Yorke - playing with people like Beckham, Scholes, Giggs and the rest of them must be a goalscorer's dream.
Some people say Van Nistelrooy is up there with the very best they've ever had at United. I wouldn't say that, but I do think he's a top-class striker.

Thierry Henry

If Van Nistelrooy is the goalscorer, Thierry Henry is the complete player. He's got the lot and he knows how to punish defenders. He has pace, tricks and plenty of skill. He scores goals and he makes them for the people around him.
It's hard to believe that he went to Arsenal as a winger, but full credit to Arsene Wenger, he spotted an out and out striker in Henry and he's been rewarded with the goals. I'm sure Henry knew he was a striker, because you always know if you have that killer instinct.

Henry must be a nightmare for defenders, because he's just so quick and you can see why the fans love him. They always love entertainers - especially entertainers who score goals.
Henry helped Arsenal to the double in the 2001/2002 season and he seems to be getting better, so I think he'll win plenty more medals.

Michael Owen

Michael Owen burst on to the scene at such a young age that it's sometimes easy to forget he's still a young man. He's a great striker and even though some people say his game is all about pace, I think there's more to him than that. Think back to that great goal against Argentina in the 1998 World Cup - that showed great skill and technique.

Like most strikers, he scores goals in fits and starts and when he has bad patches, people like to write him off. But he always bounces back and when he gets one goal, he's always likely to get a hat-trick.
Having said that Michael's game is about more than pace, he is very quick and he runs straight at defenders, which they hate.

The thing he has to do, at Liverpool and for England, is find the right partner. Then we'll see the best of Michael Owen. They always say that the best strikers hunt in pairs and Michael needs to forge the right partnership.
Alan Shearer had Teddy Sheringham, and before that Gary Lineker had Peter Beardsley, but I'm still not sure about Owen's best partner. They've tried Emile Heskey, but then he gets played wide on the left, so the search goes on.
When Michael is played alongside the right man, whoever that may be, he'll show the critics just how good he really is.

Robbie Fowler

One man who did look like he could partner Michael Owen was Robbie Fowler. He's had a bit of a lean spell since leaving Liverpool and didn't really find his best form at Leeds.
But now he's with Manchester City, I think we'll start to see Fowler at his best again and that's great news for England. He's a fantastic finisher and just has that natural instinct to go for goal.

Like every striker he needs the right service and I think he'll get that at City. It must be brilliant being a striker in a Kevin Keegan team, because everything is geared up to scoring goals.
I think Keegan must have told Fowler: "I can get you back in the England side' and I think he can. Robbie needs a settled spell with his new club and he'll be hoping to link up well with Anelka.
A lot of people have written Robbie off now, but as the old saying goes: "Form is temporary but class is permanent." He's got years ahead of him yet and he'll score plenty more goals.

Kevin Phillips

If Van Nistelrooy has the best possible support at Manchester United, the same cannot be said about Kevin Phillips. He's had to graft for his goals at Sunderland and that's what makes his record all the more impressive. Kevin is an instinctive finisher and might have been an England regular if he'd been playing at a more fashionable club. Perhaps a bit like myself, he's decided to stay loyal to his club and that's worked against him.

Just like I had Mutchy in my early days at Wolves and the partnership just clicked straight away, Phillips had a great link-up with Niall Quinn. Big Quinny was the perfect partner for someone like Kevin and things haven't been the same since he retired.

I still think Kevin Phillips has plenty of Premier League goals left in him, but they might not come at the Stadium of Light. If he does decide to move on, there will be no shortage of interest.

Gianfranco Zola

I have mixed feelings about the high number of foreigners playing in the Premier League and in England generally. Of course there are some great players now plying their trade in this country, but a lot of very ordinary players have also been brought in.

Gianfranco Zola could never be labelled 'ordinary' and he's been the perfect ambassador for the overseas players.
He's a great player, a shining example to the youngsters and he plays the game in the right spirit. He always has a smile on his face, but that doesn't mean he's messing about. You can tell he desperately wants to win.
He's only a small bloke, but he's happy to tough it out with defenders. He's an entertainer and if they spend all afternoon kicking him, he's likely to leave them looking stupid with one piece of skill.

You can tell with certain players that they just love football and Zola clearly does. He loves to entertain, he loves to score goals and he has a brilliant footballing brain.
He's one of those strikers who brings other people into the game, but he gets his fair share of goals as well. A special player.

Wayne Rooney

The new kid on the block is Everton's Wayne Rooney. Like most people, I haven't seen a great deal of him yet, but what I have seen looks promising enough.
He's powerful, quick and he likes to go straight for goal. A lot has happened to him in a short space of time and it will be interesting to see how that affects him.
But if he doesn't let it turn his head and he keeps working hard in training, he could be a big player for England for years to come.

The pressure must be massive at the moment, because of all the coverage he's had. If he can cope with that, he'll do well. But it's not about surprising defenders as an unknown teenager, it's about banging the goals in year in and year out. So it will be a while before we know just how good Wayne Rooney is.

James Beattie

It might seem strange to include James Beattie in my list of top strikers in the Premiership, especially when you look at some of the players I've missed out. But I like the look of Beattie and I can see why people are saying he's in the Alan Shearer mould.

He's a big lad and, just like Shearer, he has a physical presence that can really trouble defenders. I think that's why he won his England call-up, because we're still looking to replace Shearer at international level.

Beattie started out at Blackburn, but didn't quite make the grade there. But he's proved a few people wrong at Southampton and Gordon Strachan seems to have got the best out of him. It's a credit to Beattie that he overcame the early disappointment and never lost faith in his own ability.

One thing he has to find is a bit more consistency. All strikers have their lean spells, but Beattie seems to be either red hot or stone cold. When he does have a barren spell, it lasts for too long and that's something he needs to work on.

Pictured here with sons Joe, then aged four, and Jack, then aged seven, after receiving an MBE at an investiture ceremony at Buckingham Palace.

Chapter 14

A DAY AT THE PALACE

Memorable moments off the pitch

First you bow, then you shake hands. But don't try doing both at the same time - or you might end up head-butting Her Majesty!

When it comes to the Royal Family, everything has to be done properly, so I knew I had to be on my best behaviour when I attended Buckingham Palace to receive my MBE.

Steve Bull MBE, would you believe it! I must admit it's taken me quite a while to get used to, but I think I've finally managed it. These days, I even add the letters when anyone asks for an autograph. After all, when you've been given such an honour, why shouldn't people be aware of it?

If the idea has grown on me over the past few years, though, I still vividly recall the day when I went to London to meet the Queen. Quite honestly, I can barely explain just how I felt. I suppose it was a mixture of fear and excitement.

I travelled down with my family the previous afternoon and stayed overnight in a hotel near Lord's cricket ground, but I was so wound up about the occasion, I hardly slept a wink all night.

Even when I made my England debut, I wasn't so nervous as I was about the prospect of coming face to face with the Queen for 20 seconds.

My big worry, I think, was that there would be so many posh people around, but once I went through the Palace gates, I started to feel more at ease. It suddenly dawned on me that people from all walks of life are recognised in the New Year's Honours List.

The first thing that happened was that we were all separated into different groups, depending on which honour we had been given.

Then the big moment arrived and we went up in turn to receive our medals. I was joking, of course, about head-butting the Queen, but I swear a couple of other people almost did it, simply because they were so nervous.

"Bull, Stephen George, footballer. Used to be a tatter"

Standing right behind Her Majesty was a guy who announced our names and why we had been recognised. In my case it was for services to football, an honour of which I'm extremely proud, and I remember the Queen commenting on how I had stayed for so long at one club and asking me how many goals I'd scored.

But whenever I tell anyone about the day, I always give a slightly different version of events. I tell people that when I was announced, the man said: "Bull, Stephen George, footballer. Used to be a tatter," and that after I bowed, the Queen whispered in my ear: "I can't believe you played for the Albion!"

Anyway, once the ceremony was over, we went outside to have some photos taken, and then headed home. If it was all pretty simple and straightforward, though, I couldn't have been more proud to have been given such an honour.

These things don't just happen, of course. Someone first has to nominate you for an award, and I'm more than grateful to avid Wolves stalwart Evelyn Baker for making the Palace aware of me. Evelyn is a steward at Molineux and she always asked me to wave to her at every home match.

I know she did a lot of campaigning on my behalf, and I was obviously delighted that all her efforts were rewarded.

The first I knew about it was when a letter arrived from the Prime Minister, saying my services to the game had been recognised and that I'd been awarded the MBE.

Then I had to keep quiet until the announcement was officially made - which took a fair bit of doing.

Receiving another fantastic welcome at Molineux

Another memorable occasion away from the football pitch was when a 'This Is Your Life' evening was organised for me. Maybe the setting wasn't quite as regal, and there was certainly no tap on the shoulder from Michael Aspel, like you see on the television programme of the same name. But I felt very proud when something like 2,000 people packed into Wolverhampton Civic Hall to hear about my career.

Among those who talked about me were Sid Day, the man who got me into professional football, Tipton Town secretary John Cross and a number of people who I'd known so well during my years at Molineux.

There was Graham Turner - my first Wolves manager - John Richards, the man whose goalscoring record I broke, plus past team-mates Andy Thompson, Andy Mutch and Robbie Dennison and former England goalkeeper Peter Shilton.
One of Wolves' most ardent supporters, Rob McNally, also had a few words to say, and at times it was a bit embarrassing listening to so many complimentary things about myself - particularly as some of them weren't true! Thankfully, I didn't have to say a great deal myself. I left that to the various guests and Bob Hall of Central TV, who hosted the event.

"At times it was a bit embarrassing, particularly as some of them weren't true!"

The evening was part of my testimonial year, which featured numerous other functions organised by my committee chairman Jim Cadman.
Jim organised a lunch, a dinner and a golf day, plus personal appearances at pubs and clubs around the area, and an emotional year came to a conclusion with a game against Santos at Molineux.
Even though it was only a friendly match, it was another new experience for me to play against players whose flair I'd seen on television over the years. If it hadn't been for my testimonial, I would never have had the chance of playing against the boys from Brazil.

Coming to terms with the decision to
call it a day during the pre-season tour
of Sweden, 13 July 1999.

Chapter 15

HOW WILL I MANAGE?
Retirement and the future

It was one of the toughest decisions I've ever had to make, but in the end there was only one option. During Wolves' pre-season tour of Sweden in July, 1999, I came to the realisation that my knees just weren't going to carry me through another season of First Division football. It was time to hang up my boots.

When we flew out to Sweden, I was hopeful of giving it another go, even though I'd undergone three operations during the previous two years and had hardly played at all in the 1998-99 campaign.

But it soon became apparent that I would have to retire. I was gutted, but there was really no other choice. My knee started to swell up, and although our physio Barry Holmes put some ice on it, it was even bigger a couple of hours later. I could hardly bend it, and Barry gave me an ultimatum. I was going to need another operation no matter what happened, but he warned that trying to carry on playing would be a massive gamble because I would be risking permanent damage. He was straight with me, saying that although the decision was mine, he thought it was wiser to knock things on the head.

It was what I'd been expecting, so his advice didn't come as a complete surprise, but it was still a blow to know my career was over after 16 years, most of them at Molineux. Maybe I could have tried to carry on for another six months, but I would just have been kidding both myself and the fans, and I didn't want that. I wanted to finish at the top.

Once the decision had been made, I spoke to manager Colin Lee, who told me I was welcome to stay on for the rest of the tour. That's what I did, and at least I made myself useful by doing some massage on the other lads. I have strong hands, so they were all queuing up for a massage, even though I'd never done it before.

All the same, it was hard to watch my team-mates training and playing matches when all I could manage was a few sit-ups - and look back over some great times with Wolves.

It also crossed my mind that my retirement might have been avoided if I hadn't always been so keen to play, even when not fully fit. When you are knocking in the goals, you just want to keep playing, and I have to admit I turned out a fair few times when I wasn't 100 per cent.

"I enjoyed every minute of my career, and I wouldn't have changed it for anything"

There were occasions when I had strained or pulled muscles, but I ignored them if I felt I could get through a game. If I'd been a bit more careful, and been willing to sit out the odd game, I'm convinced I could have played on for another 12 or 18 months.

But I'm not complaining. I enjoyed every minute of my career, and I wouldn't have changed it for anything. I had nearly 13 great years with Wolves, and the only disappointment was that we never made it to the Premiership while I was there. Sometimes I look back and wonder if I could have been successful in the top flight with another club, but that's all ifs and buts, and I was happy with what I had. It was just disappointing that I wasn't able to help Wolves into the Premiership, because I'd desperately wanted to finish the job I'd started a decade earlier when my goals carried us to two consecutive promotions.

But now the decision had been taken, it was time to start looking forward rather than back. Once we returned from Sweden, I went into hospital to have my knee cleaned out, and then had six weeks of rehabilitation. During that period, I just tried to keep myself as fit as possible because it was still in the back on my mind that a comeback might be possible - although I knew I was only kidding myself.

Even so, I remained on Wolves' playing staff until the following June, when my contract expired, although my input was restricted to public relations work on behalf of the club.

Player/Coach at Hereford Utd,
March 2001.

I was still involved with the team to a certain extent, and I always made a point of going into the dressing room on match days to wish them all the best. But most of my time was spent meeting and greeting supporters in the various executive boxes and disabled areas around Molineux. I can't deny that I enjoyed it, either. Obviously it was never going to beat playing football, but I had a laugh with the people I met and the fact that I was spending 10 minutes of my time with them seemed to mean a lot to them. Thankfully, I had plenty of stories to tell, so there was never any danger of running out of things to say.

That side of things continued once I was no longer registered as a player, the club giving me a 10-hours-a-week PR contract, but I was itching to be involved in the game again, and about a year later I got a coaching position with Hereford United under Graham Turner. Graham, of course, had been my first Wolves boss, and it was working with him that got me thinking about a management job for myself.

Being involved with football day in day out made me realise just how much I fancied the idea of becoming a manager, and that's still my target.
For the time being, I'm happy enough running my new business, Steve Bull Enterprises, which involves anything from personal appearances to selling limited edition prints, and that's something I would like to keep going even if I get another job in football.

But there's no denying that my priority is to manage a club, and I think I learned enough from 16 years as a player and that spell with Graham Turner at Hereford to know what's required. I know footballers inside out - how they think, what makes them tick, everything - so I reckon I have a lot to offer.
Obviously I'm not daft enough to think I'm going to land a top job straight away, but I would be more than happy to gain some experience at a non-League club. If I can get my foot in the door, though, I will be aiming high. I got to the top the hard way as a player, so I'm sure I can do it again.

Chapter 16

WHAT THEY SAY ABOUT BULLY

Stuart Pearce

Steve was an old-fashioned, very robust centre forward. His style drew much influence from players of the fifties. A player of immense honesty which led him to ten superb years with Wolves. I spent a few years in the England squad with Steve, including the Italia '90 World Cup campaign. He was unlucky not to have played more matches - simply because of the Lineker / Beardsley partnership that was doing so well at the time.

The biggest accolade I can bestow on Bully is that he was the type of player I would have liked in my team. Steve always gave 100% commitment, was as brave as a lion on the pitch whilst remaining extremely loyal to his football club - a rare commodity in this day and age.

George Best

As a youngster I had the pleasure of seeing the great Wolves team of the fifties which included many superb players like Bill Slater, the legendary Billy Wright, Ron Flowers, Peter Broadbent and Jimmy Mullen. As I look back now, only one other Wolves player, in my opinion, could improve on that great team – Steve Bull. He was a revelation for the Wolves with his amazing goalscoring exploits and total dedication to the club, both on and off the field.

Ian Rush

Steve consistently scored goals for Wolves, rarely experiencing a really lean spell. This alone would have made him a valuable asset to any club in the country, but despite great interest from other clubs, Steve remained with a club he still has a great affection for even to this day. I have always admired Steve for this and fully understand why he remains a great idol by the Black Country fans.

Bully was always an out and out striker, in many ways like Malcolm MacDonald or Stan Collymore in their heyday. Steve was a powerful striker, always difficult to stop once they are running with the ball and liable to shoot from anywhere at anytime - something that no goalkeeper relishes!

Bryan Robson

The England versus Scotland game at Hampden Park will always remind me of Steve's potential at International level. Although it marked his first international appearance, coming on as a substitute, Steve certainly left his mark, destroying the Scots in the process!

Steve was always a model professional at both club and international level, and it's still not difficult to see why he is so revered by the Wolves' supporters.

John Richards

Steve had a natural instinctive gift for goal scoring. He gave the fans what they expect from a player wearing a Wolves shirt – total commitment.

**STEVE
BULL**
The Memoirs of
WOLVES

Charles Ross
Editor, A Load of Bull

Wolves have arguably never had another player quite like Bully. Sacrificing career advancement and financial gain, Bully repeatedly proved to be a major force in Wolves' climb back from the footballing doldrums.Put quite simply, Bully gave it everything, and all for Wolves. I count myself priviledged to have stood on the South Bank then, and the Billy Wright stand in later years, to watch the wonderful achievements that Bully orchestrated unfurl before our very eyes.

Steve has always been one of our own, a local lad raised on the same streets, where as youngsters we all aspired to have the same effect on the Wolves that Bully has achieved in reality. A generation from now our children and grandchildren will ask "what was Bully like?" The videos will be there to capture the goals - but to saviour the emotion of it all, you really had to be there...

Sir Stanley Matthews

Steve was amazing. He seemed to get quicker every season and he reminded me of the great pre-war Arsenal centre-forward Ted drake. I can pay 'Bully' no greater compliment than that. *Spoken in 1997 before his death.*

Ron Atkinson

Steve was one of the few players I wanted to sign as a manager. But I simply could not lure him away from Molineux – he basically loved playing and scoring goals for Wolves.

Graham Turner

Courage, strength and determination were the attributes which would brush aside defenders and result in him getting a strike on goal – and the vast majority of his efforts would finish in the back of the net. It was a thrill to see him in full flight with defenders trailing in his wake. I had the greatest respect for him as a man and as a professional footballer. He will remain synonymous with the revival of Wolverhampton Wanderers Football Club.

Les Ferdinand

Over several years I have enjoyed a great rapport with the fans, be it at non-league Hayes, QPR, Newcastle or Tottenham. But I cannot recall a player who has enjoyed a better relationship with his fans than Steve Bull.

There are many who believe a striker has all the glory, but that's not necessarily true. Fans can be very demanding and you have to work hard to earn their respect and maintain it. In a way, I understand why Steve remained lyal and stayed with Wolves when opportunities may have arisen to go elsewhere. It could be said that he may have won more England caps had he taken his talents into the Premiership, but there is no substitute for happiness.

His goal scoring record have ensured he goes down as the most prolific striker in Wolves' history. But I'm sure that he will be remembered for more than just the goals by the fans, and let us not forget that at the end of the day they are the ones that count.

In action against Spurs
in the FA Cup Fourth Round,
in 1996

Chapter 17
BULL'S GOALS
all 32∅ of them...

For West Bromwich Albion:

1 13 September 1986 v. Ipswich Town (h) League Division 1 (lost 3-4)
Bully's first competitive goal came in the 20th minute of the thrilling encounter at The Hawthorns. Scot Bobby Williamson collected a pass from Steve Mackenzie and fed the ball through to 'Bully' who scored with a rasping right-footed drive from 15 yards.

2 13 September 1986 v. Ipswich Town (h) League Division 1 (lost 3-4)
In the 54th minute, with Albion leading 2-1, left-back David Burrows drilled a splendid long through ball to 'Bully' who calmly slotted past 'keeper Paul Cooper.

3 24 September 1986 v. Derby County (a) Milk Cup 2nd round 1st leg (lost 1-4)
Albion took the lead in the sixth minute when 'Bully' burst through the County defence, collected Martyn Bennett's pass and neatly lobbed the ball over 'keeper Mark Wallington.

★ Bully also scored in a penalty shoot-out, 13 November 1985 v. Chelsea (h) Full Members Cup, Southern Area semi-final
(lost 4-5 after 2-2 draw)

For Wolverhampton Wanderers:

1 2 December 1986 v. Cardiff City (a) Freight Rover Trophy Preliminary round (won 1-0).
After a 75th minute aerial challenge with City defender Terry Boyle, 'Bully' reacted quickest as the ball dropped down and he lashed a powerful right-foot shot past 'keeper Graham Moseley...with Boyle holding his face!

2 13 December 1986 v. Hartlepool United (a) League Division 4 (won 1-0)
In the 25th minute 'Bully' raced onto Jon Purdie's through ball, rounded 'keeper Eddie Blackburn and scored comfortably from close range.

3 16 December 1986 v. AFC Bournemouth (h) Freight Rover Trophy Preliminary round (won 4-3)
Using his strength, 'Bully' brushed aside Mark Whitlock's 38th minute challenge to beat 'keeper Gerry Peyton comfortably from eight yards.

4 16 December 1986 v. AFC Bournemouth (h) Freight Rover Trophy Preliminary round (won 4-3)
Paul Dougherty's low cross was missed by Andy Mutch but the alert 'Bully' was there to apply the finishing touch in the 55th minute.

5 20 December 1986 v. Southend United (h) League Division 4 (lost 1-2)
A late consolation goal, scored in the 86th minute when 'Bully' turned in Paul Dougherty's sweeping cross.

6 27 December 1986 v. Exeter City (h) League Division 4 (drew 2-2)
Gaining possession some 40 yards out, 'Bully' charged past centre-half Shaun Taylor and after cutting in from the left, he scored with a fierce low drive on eight minutes.

7 24 January 1987 v. Cardiff City (a) League Division 4 (won 2-0)
Three minutes before half-time 'Bully' darted through the middle to lash a sweet right footer past 'keeper Mel Rees.

8 7 February 1987 v. Stockport County (h) League Division 4 (won 3-1).
Spotting goalkeeper Andy Gorton off his line, 'Bully' superbly lobbed home Wolves' clinching goal in the 88th minute.

9 3 March 1987 v. Colchester United (h) League Division 4 (won 2-0)
Floyd Streete fed 'Bully' with a long pass; the ball was switched out to Andy Mutch and there was 'Bully' in the centre to smack the return into the net and sew up the points with four minutes remaining.

10 7 March 1987 v. Leyton Orient (a) League Division 4 (lost 1-3)
As the ball ran free inside the home penalty area, 'Bully' was on to it like a flash and netted low past 'keeper Peter Wells from close range (57 minutes).

11 28 March 1987 v. Scunthorpe United (h) League Division 4 (won 1-0)
In the 28th minute 'Bully' timed his run and dive perfectly to head Robbie Dennison's pin-point cross past stranded 'keeper Ron Green.

12 18 April 1987 v. Peterborough United (a) League Division 4 (won 1-0)
Jon Purdie headed on 'keeper Mark Kendall's long clearance for 'Bully' to charge through the middle and crash a volley past Kevin Shoemake in the Posh goal.

13   2 May 1987 v. Lincoln City (h) League Division 4 (won 3-0)
The alert 'Bully' latched onto Shane Nicholson's weak back pass to score easily on two minutes.

14   2 May 1987 v. Lincoln City (h) League Division 4 (won 3-0)
A well-timed run took 'Bully' clear of the Imps' defence as he controlled Robert Kelly's pass before slotting the ball comfortably
past Lee Butler in the 12th minute.

15   4 May 1987 v. Exeter City (a) League Division 4 (won 3-1)
Andy Thompson knocked down Steve Stoutt's measured free-kick for 'Bully' to shoot low past 'keeper John Shaw in the 12th minute.

16   9 May 1987 v. Hartlepool United (h) League Division 4 (won 4-1)
On the half-hour mark 'Bully' battled his way past two defenders before unleashing a thumping drive high into the 'Pool net .

17   9 May 1987 v. Hartlepool United (h) League Division 4 (won 4-1)
With 86 minutes played, the score at 2-1 and Wolves under pressure, 'Bully' raced into the box and cracked home a beauty
to bring the fans racing onto the pitch.

18   9 May 1987 v. Hartlepool United (h) League Division 4 (won 4-1)
Bully completed his first hat-trick for Wolves with two minutes remaining, gleefully slipping the ball into the net after neat
build-up play involving Andy Thompson and Wayne Clarke.

19   17 May 1987 v. Colchester United (a) Play-off semi-final, 1st leg (won 2-0)
Bully was on hand in the 32nd minute to fire the loose ball past Alex Chamberlain after Andy Thompson's angled drive
had bounced back off an upright

20   15 August 1987 v. Scarborough (a) League Division 4 (drew 2-2)
In the 29th minute Phil Robinson, after gaining possession in midfield, fed the ball through to 'Bully' who sped past Ian Bennyworth
before crashing his shot 'past 'keeper Kevin Blackwell.

21   25 August 1987 v. Notts County (a) Littlewoods Cup, 1st round, 2nd leg (won 2-1)
Just before the hour mark, Andy Mutch chested Keith Downing's cross into 'Bully's path and the striker duly added the finishing touch.

22   25 August 1987 v. Notts County (a) Littlewoods Cup, 1st round, 2nd leg (won 2-1)
Clear inside the penalty area with 10 minutes remaining, 'Bully' chose to lob 'keeper Mick Leonard whose outstretched arm
failed to keep the ball out.

23   29 August 1987 v. Hereford United (a) League Division 4 (won 2-1).
After collecting a long through ball, 'Bully' outpaced Gary Stevens before slamming the ball high into the Hereford net
past 'keeper Kevin Rose in the 16th minute.

24   31 August 1987 v. Scunthorpe United (h) League Division 4 (won 4-1)
Keith Downing's precise left-wing cross in the 9th minute was headed firmly into the 'Iron's' net by the high-fling 'Bully'.

25   31 August 1987 v. Scunthorpe United (h) League Division 4 (won 4-1)
Taking the ball in his stride after a long clearance, 'Bully' let fly from 15 yards to beat 'keeper Ron Green all ends up with
eight minutes remaining.

26   5 September 1987 v. Cardiff City (a) League Division 4 (lost 2-3)
A curling right-wing cross on 54 minutes from Andy Thompson was stabbed home by 'Bully' as the City defence hesitated.

27   12 September 1987 v. Crewe Alexandra (h) League Division 4 (drew 2-2)
After a swift one-two with Jon Purdie, 'Bully' neatly swept home his eighth goal of the season in the 6th minute.

28   16 September 1987 v. Peterborough United (a) League Division 4 (drew 1-1)
In the 24th minute Floyd Streete hurled a long throw towards 'Bully' who controlled the ball before turning his marker
to bury an unstoppable shot past 'keeper Joe Neenan.

29 22 September 1987 v. Manchester City (a) Littlewoods Cup, 2nd round 1st leg (won 2-1)
In the 55th minute Phil Robinson fed Andy Mutch who in turn slipped the ball into 'Bully's path; he went on to
drill a powerful shot past Eric Nixon.

30 26 September 1987 v. Torquay United (h) League Division 4 (lost 1-2)
Torquay's 'keeper Kenny Allen beat out Andy Thompson's close-range effort but the alert 'Bully' pounced to net a late consolation goal
for Wolves in the 88th minute.

31 29 September 1987 v. Rochdale (h) League Division 4 (won 2-0)
Following Keith Downing's 77th minute cross from the left, Andy Mutch had a shot beaten away, Bully fired the return
against an upright but then swooped to put away the rebound.

32 10 October 1987 v. Carlisle United (a) League Division 4 (won 1-0)
Beating the offside trap, Andy Mutch crossed from the right for 'Bully', charging between defenders, to fire a shot at goal.
'Keeper Martin Taylor managed to get his hands on the ball but couldn't prevent it crossing the line.

33 17 October 1987 v. Tranmere Rovers (h) League Division 4 (won 3-0)
In the 23rd minute 'Bully' latched onto Keith Downing's long accurate pass before lashing his shot past 'keeper Billy O'Rourke
from the edge of the penalty-area.

34 20 October 1987 v. Cambridge United (h) League Division 4 (won 3-0)
Taking Robbie Dennison's pass, 'Bully' brushed aside a challenge from Gary Poole, before smartly placing a right-foot shot
wide of keeper Keith Branagan in the 12th minute.

35 27 October 1987 v. Swansea City (a) Freight Rover Trophy, Preliminary round (drew 1-1)
Behind with seven minutes to play, 'Bully' earned his side a draw with a brilliant individual goal, netting with a fierce cross-shot
past 'keeper Mike Hughes after nut-megging a defender near the touchline.

36 3 November 1987 v. Swansea City (a) League Division 4 (won 2-1)
Wrestling clear of defender Alan Knill, 'Bully' composed himself before beating 'keeper Hughes with a well-struck shot in the 28th minute.

37 14 November 1987 v. Cheltenham Town (h) FA Cup 1st round (won 5-1)
In the 27th minute 'Bully' burst through the centre of the Cheltenham defence before smashing the ball right-footed into the
top far corner of the net from 18 yards.

38 14 November 1987 v. Cheltenham Town (h) FA Cup 1st round (won 5-1)
On the hour mark, goalkeeper Churchwood saved Andy Mutch's powerful header but was left stranded as
Bully whipped in the rebound with an angled shot.

39 14 November 1987 v. Cheltenham Town (h) FA Cup 1st round (won 5-1)
Nigel Vaughan did the spadework and 'Bully' finished things off with a thumping left-footer with six minutes remaining
to complete his first FA Cup hat-trick.

40 24 November 1987 v. Bristol City (h) Freight Rover Trophy, Preliminary round (won 3-1)
On 40 minutes Andy Mutch and Robbie Dennison linked up down the right and from the latter's cross Bully put the ball beyond
'keeper Mark Prudhoe with sweet aplomb.

41 24 November 1987 v. Bristol City (h) Freight Rover Trophy, Preliminary round (won 3-1)
Mutch created the 76th minute opening which 'Bully' took competently with a well-struck shot.

42 19 December 1987 v. Leyton Orient (h) League Division 4 (won 2-0)
Bully opening the scoring in the 58th minute with a hard, low drive from 15 yards after a smart build-up.

43 19 December 1987 v. Leyton Orient (h) League Division 4 (won 2-0)
With ten minutes remaining 'Bully' rose unchallenged to net with a deft header to tie up the points.

44 1 January 1988 v. Hereford United (h) League Division 4 (won 2-0)
In the 39th minute 'Bully' broke the deadlock by scoring with a cracking drive from 12 yards after superbly turning his marker on the run.

Avoiding the attentions of Nottingham Forest's
Des Walker, January 1992

BULLY'S GOALS

45 1 January 1988 v. Hereford United (h) League Division 4 (won 2-0)
After a smart build-up involving three players, Bully showed confidence and composure by picking his spot before firing the ball past 'keeper Kevin Rose.

46 19 January 1988 v. Brentford (h) Sherpa Van Trophy 1st round (won 4-0)
In the 9th minute 'Bully' brushed away Keith Millen's challenge before blasting home a shot inside 'keeper Gary Phillips' near post

47 19 January 1988 v. Brentford (h) Sherpa Van Trophy 1st round (won 4-0)
Bully scored his second goal of the game in the 77th minute, knocking in the rebound after Phillips had saved Robbie Dennison's initial header.

48 19 January 1988 v. Brentford (h) Sherpa Van Trophy 1st round (won 4-0)
Another hat-trick…and 'Bully' clinched it in the 85th minute with a marvellous 20-yarder which he celebrated Brazilian-style, charging round with his arms out wide.

49 6 February 1988 v. Cardiff City (h) League Division 4 (lost1-4)
Turning smartly inside the area, 'Bully' beat veteran 'keeper George Wood with a well-struck shot from 12 yards.

50 9 February 1988 v. Peterborough United (h) Sherpa Van Trophy 2nd round (won 4-0)
Nigel Vaughan's 4th minute corner was not cleared and 'Bully', alert and free, belted the ball high into the net from close range.

51 9 February 1988 v. Peterborough United (h) Sherpa Van Trophy 2nd round (won 4-0)
On 52 minutes Andy Mutch did the spadework, 'Posh' defender Steve Collins flapped and 'Bully' pounced to smash the ball high into the net with venom.

52 13 February 1988 v. Exeter City (a) League Division 4 (won 4-2)
Looking up, Andy Mutch delivered a magnificent 7th minute cross which 'Bully' headed home in style past 'keeper Mel Gwinnett

53 13 February 1988 v. Exeter City (a) League Division 4 (won 4-2)
Gary Bellamy raced down the right in the 32nd minute before crossing low for Andy Mutch to switch play to Bully who hooked the ball delightfully past Gwinnett as he fell.

54 13 February 1988 v. Exeter City (a) League Division 4 (won 4-2)
Bully somehow bundled the ball over the line in the 61st minute after Robbie Dennison's pass had been miscued by Mutch causing 'keeper Gwinnett to lose his composure.

55 27 February 1988 v. Bolton Wanderers (h) League Division 4 (won 4-0)
On loan full-back Bobby McDonald's long ball was helped on by Mutch to Bully who scored with a right-footed stunner past 'keeper David Felgate to give his side a 6th minute lead.

56 27 February 1988 v. Bolton Wanderers (h) League Division 4 (won 4-0)
Mark Came charged down Andy Mutch's shot only for 'Bully' to pounce with a booming shot from close range in the 22nd minute.

57 8 March 1988 v. Torquay United (h) Sherpa Van Trophy, area semi-final (won 1-0)
The game was decided in the 18th minute when 'Bully' drifted forward to glance Robbie Dennison's right-wing cross past Kenny Allen.

58 26 March 1988 v. Darlington (h) League Division 4 (won 5-3)
As defender Gary Morgan hesitated, 'Bully' seized his chance in the 40th minute, hammering the ball past 'keeper Keith Granger from the edge of the area.

59 26 March 1988 v. Darlington (h) League Division 4 (won 5-3)
Mutch headed down Dennison's precise cross from the left for 'Bully' to smash a shot past Granger in the 67th minute.

60 26 March 1988 v. Darlington (h) League Division 4 (won 5-3)
Bully completed his hat-trick when he raced clear of the Quakers' defence to fire an unstoppable shot past the advancing 'keeper.

61 2 April 1988 v. Burnley (a) League Division 4 (won 3-0)
Gary Bellamy's right-wing free-kick was not cleared and 'Bully', alert as always pounced to smash home a 15-yard volley in the 61st minute to make it 2-0.

62 4 April 1988 v. Colchester United (h) League Division 4 (won 2-0)
Phil Chard's 10th minute throw-in was flicked on by Andy Mutch for 'Bully' who in a flash whipped the ball low past 'keeper Craig Forrest.

63 4 April 1988 v. Colchester United (h) League Division 4 (won 2-0)
Bully set a new Wolves scoring record (for most goals in a season) when, in the 75th minute, he took a short pass from Nigel Vaughan, held off weak challenges from two defenders before firing hard and low past a static Forrest.

64 12 April 1988 v. Notts County (a) Sherpa Van Trophy area Final 1st leg (drew 1-1)
A poor clearance by County defender Paul Smalley was collected by Bully who beat 'keeper Mick Leonard with a vicious half-volley in the 61st minute.

65 19 April 1988 v. Notts County (h) Sherpa Van Trophy Area Final 2nd leg (won 3-0)
In front of 18,413 fans 'Bully' opened the scoring on eight minutes when he accepted Micky Holmes' delightful pass before shooting right-footed past the helpless Leonard.

66 19 April 1988 v. Notts County (h) Sherpa Van Trophy Area Final 2nd leg (won 3-0)
Floyd Streete's long throw-in was touched on by Andy Mutch for 'Bully' whose strength took him past defenders Paul Hart and Chris Withe before finishing with a blistering shot past the bemused Leonard.

67 23rd April 1988 v. Swansea City (h) League Division 4 (won 2-0)
In the 50th minute Andy Mutch carried the ball fully 40 yards from deep in his own half before freeing 'Bully' who went on to score with a smart right-footer from just inside the area.

68 26 April 1988 v. Newport County (a) League Division 4 (won 3-1)
A crowd of just 3,409 saw 'Bully' have an easy tap-in from four yards in the 21st minute after Phil Chard had headed Steve Stoutt's free-kick across the goalmouth.

69 26 April 1988 v. Newport County (a) League Division 4 (won 3-1)
Bully brought up his half-century of goals for the season with a neat left-footed volley (from Keith Downing's measured cross) in the 25th minute.

70 2 May 1988 v. Hartlepool United (h) League Division 4 (won 2-0)
In the 10th minute Bully scored a great goal - netting with an overhead kick, created out of nothing from a bouncing ball inside the area.

71 2 May 1988 v. Hartlepool United (h) League Division 4 (won 2-0)
In the last minute of the game Bully, leaving his markers yards behind him, raced into the Hartlepool danger-zone before slamming the ball past 'keeper Kevin Carr.

72 30 August 1988 v. Birmingham City (h) Littlewoods Cup, 1st round 1st leg (won 3-2)
Bully, finding just enough space, rose to head home Robbie Dennison's cross in the 50th minute.

73 30 August 1988 v. Birmingham City (h) Littlewoods Cup, 1st round 1st leg (won 3-2)
A lucky one here...Dennison's 81st minute shot struck the right boot of Blues 'keeper Tony Godden and then bounced off the onrushing 'Bully' and into the unguarded net.

74 20 September 1988 v. Aldershot (h) League Division 3 (won 1-0)
Bully toe-ended his first League goal of the season in the 27th minute...being in the right place at the right time after Andy Mutch's intended pass had struck a defender.

75 24 September 1988 v. Swansea City (a) League Division 3 (won 5-2)
Three minutes before half-time 'Bully' controlled a bouncing ball inside the Swans' penalty area, turned and finished in style.

76 24 September 1988 v. Swansea City (a) League Division 3 (won 5-2)
In the 58th minute, the unmarked 'Bully' headed in Robbie Dennison's corner kick for his side's fifth goal.

77 1 October 1988 v. Port Vale (h) League Division 3 (drew 3-3)
Nine minutes on the clock and Andy Mutch's precise cross from the right was perfectly put away by the lurking Bully against second-placed Port Vale.

78 1 October 1988 v. Port Vale (h) League Division 3 (drew 3-3)
It was Robbie Dennison who provided the cross this time, allowing Bully to slide in ahead of three Vale defenders to get the final touch in the 88th minute to salvage a point.

79 15 October 1988 v. Wigan Athletic (h) League Division 3 (won 2-1)
Robbie Dennison's through ball in the 31st minute completely divided the Wigan defence allowing the rampaging Bully to smash his shot beyond the diving Phil Hughes.

80 22 October 1988 v. Bolton Wanderers (a) League Division 3 (won 2-1)
Mark Kendall's long clearance in the 80th minute was helped on by Mutch to Bully who finished with a stunning left-foot drive that earned his side all three points at Burnden Park.

81 29 October 1988 v. Gillingham (a) League Division 3 (won 3-1)
After some neat footwork by his partner-in-crime Andy Mutch, Bully somehow got his knee to the ball to send it past 'keeper Phil Kite in the 87th minute to clinch victory.

82 5 November 1988 v. Southend United (h) League Division 3 (won 3-0)
Bully moved in for the kill as two Shrimpers' defenders hesitated…his left-foot finding the net in the 69th minute.

83 12 December 1988 v. Huddersfield Town (h) League Division 3 (won 4-1).
On 65 minutes the alert Bully chased after Mark Venus' long ball, touched it past 'keeper Steve Hardwick and then ran on to smash it gleefully into the net.

84 12 December 1988 v. Huddersfield Town (h) League Division 3 (won 4-1).
With almost the last kick of the game Bully found himself free inside the penalty area and he made no mistake, cracking the ball wide of the hapless Hardwick.

85 26 December 1988 v. Preston North End (h) League Division 3 (won 6-0)
There seemed little threat as Andy Mutch's 13th minute cross looped into the North End box, but Bully thought otherwise and he quickly snapped up the half-chance to beat 'keeper David Brown with a super strike.

86 26 December 1988 v. Preston North End (h) League Division 3 (won 6-0)
On the half-hour Richard Money, not noticing Bully behind him, played a weak back-pass to his 'keeper. Never-say-die Bully chased after it, won the race (ahead of the 'keeper) and scored with ease.

87 26 December 1988 v. Preston North End (h) League Division 3 (won 6-0)
Bob Atkins was robbed by Mutch who in turn fed the ball through to Bully who found the back of the net with a low perfectly executed ground shot from 10 yards (59 minutes).

88 26 December 1988 v. Preston North End (h) League Division 3 (won 6-0)
Bully completed his first 'fourtimer' with a clinical finish on 76 minutes after some splendid work down the left flank by Mark Venus and Keith Downing.

89 30 November 1988 v. Hereford United (a) Sherpa Van Trophy Preliminary round (drew 2-2).
Andy Mutch, finding space, drilled over the perfect cross, which Bully tucked away effortlessly in the 63rd minute.

90 13 December 1988 v. Port Vale (h) Sherpa Van Trophy, Preliminary round (won 5-1)
In the 10th minute Andy Mutch, meeting Mark Kendall's long clearance, flicked the ball onto Bully who went on to finish the move in style from 15 yards.

91 13 December 1988 v. Port Vale (h) Sherpa Van Trophy, Preliminary round (won 5-1)
Some neat work in the 22nd minute by Robbie Dennison and Andy Thompson saw Bully get on the end of the resulting cross to thump a header past Mark Grew.

92 13 December 1988 v. Port Vale (h) Sherpa Van Trophy, Preliminary round (won 5-1)
Dennison sent the ball squirting through the square Vale defence to Bully in the 66th minute. Taking it in his stride, the striker neatly chipped a right-footer past Grew.

I prepare to replace Gary Lineker
to make my World Cup debut
against Ireland in the World Cup
Italia '90 Group F match, June 1990

BULLY'S GOALS

93   13 December 1988 v. Port Vale (h) Sherpa Van Trophy, Preliminary round (won 5-1)
In the 74th minute, Thompson found enough space to deliver a telling cross which Bully buried past the demoralised Grew with a powerful header.

94   17 December 1988 v. Mansfield Town (h) League Division 3 (won 6-2)
Credit to Mick Gooding who in the 26th minute, created space on the flank before twisting over a precise cross which Bully diverted past 'keeper Brian Cox's right-hand with a smartly, directed header.

95   17 December 1988 v. Mansfield Town (h) League Division 3 (won 6-2)
Two minutes before half-time, Floyd Streete lifted a high ball into the Stags' penalty area. Bully went for it, lost his balance but recovered quickly to lash it high into the net from 10 yards.

96   17 December 1988 v. Mansfield Town (h) League Division 3 (won 6-2)
Gary Bellamy's high ball in the 58th minute was nudged further down field by Mutch for Bully to race onto and beat the advancing Cox with another venomous drive.

97   31 December 1988 v. Brentford (a) League Division 3 (drew 2-2)
Like he had done earlier in the year against the Bees, Bully chased after a through ball, shrugged off a challenge from defender Keith Millen before beating 'keeper Tony Parks with ease.

98   2 January 1989 v. Chester City (h) League Division 3 (won 3-1)
In the 18th minute, the tireless figure of Andy Mutch neatly teed-up a chance for Bully who, without hesitation, found the net with a marvellously executed overhead-kick.

99   10 January 1989 v. Cardiff City (h) League Division 3 (won 2-0)
After controlling Keith Downing's 35th minute cross, Bully successfully held off the challenges of three City defenders before firing in a sweet right-footer from fully 20 yards as he raced across the area.

100   24 January 1989 v. Bristol City (h) Sherpa Van Trophy 1st round (won 3-0)
After Floyd Street and Andy Mutch had carved out an opening, Bully reached the century mark with a mishit right-footed shot in the 14th minute that just about crossed the line.

101   24 January 1989 v. Bristol City (h) Sherpa Van Trophy 1st round (won 3-0)
Picking up Steve McClaren's weak 71st minute back-pass, Bully weaved round 'keeper Keith Waugh before smashing home a left-footer from the narrowest of angles.

102   24 January 1989 v. Bristol City (h) Sherpa Van Trophy 1st round (won 3-0)
Robbie Dennison's 76th minute pass found Nigel Vaughan who, in turn, weighted his cross perfectly for Bully to move in and side foot home from all of 12 yards.

103   11 February 1989 v. Fulham (h) League Division 3 (won 5-2)
Dennison crossed to the near post where Mutch turned only to see his shot blocked. The ball bounced invitingly for Bully who connected fiercely with his left foot to put Wolves ahead on six minutes.

104   11 February 1989 v. Fulham (h) League Division 3 (won 5-2)
Andy Thompson's first-time cross eluded John Marshall and fell onto the chest of Bully who quickly got the ball under control before cracking it hard and true past Jim Stannard from 15 yards.

105   11 February 1989 v. Fulham (h) League Division 3 (won 5-2)
In the 67th minute Mark Venus swung over the perfect cross that fell behind Marshall and Doug Rougvie allowing Bully to move and slip his ground shot under Stannard.

106   28 February 1989 v. Blackpool (a) League Division 3 (won 2-0)
On his own, Bully broke the deadlock in the 63rd minute when he took on and beat three home defenders before unleashing a low right-footed shot which swerved into the net past the diving Vince O'Keefe.

107   4 March 1989 v. Bolton Wanderers (h) League Division 3 (won 1-0)
A great goal to win any match…Bully's 34th minute crackerjack against Bolton came after he collected Andy Mutch's flick-on 30 yards out. He turned his man before winding up to send a left-foot Bullyet past David Felgate.

STEVE
BULL
WOLVES

108   14 March 1989 v. Gillingham (h) League Division 3 (won 6-1)
Wolves had already scored five times before Bully got in on the act in the 50th minute, charging through to bury a shot into the bottom corner of the net following Andy Mutch's intelligent flick-on from Mark Kendall's punt downfield.

109   18 March 1989 v. Bury (h) League Division 3 (won 4-0)
In the 36th minute Dennison passed to Gooding, who then chipped forward to Bully whose first touch was spot-on, allowing him to crack the ball past Simon Farnworth from just inside the penalty-area.

110   18 March 1989 v. Bury (h) League Division 3 (won 4-0)
Mutch held the ball up before feeding the overlapping Dennison down the left. His cross was perfect for Bully who almost burst the net with his powerful header from six yards range in the 50th minute.

111   18 March 1989 v. Bury (h) League Division 3 (won 4-0)
Bully registered yet another hat-trick with one of the easiest goals of his career - a simple tap-in from just two yards out after 'keeper Farnworth had fumbled Thompson's tempting cross.

112   22 March 1989 v. Hereford United (a) Sherpa Van Trophy, second round (won 2-0)
Mutch sent Bully bursting forward. The striker lost control momentarily but regained possession and thanks to a lucky rebound off Andy Crane, somehow managed to squeeze the ball past 'keeper Tony Elliott.

113   1 April 1989 v. Mansfield Town (a) League Division 3 (lost 1-3)
After 30 minutes play Robbie Dennison's delicate chip over the defence sent Bully scurrying forward. He made no mistake with a powerful shot into the corner of Brian Cox's net.

114   8 April 1989 v. Brentford (h) League Division 3 (won 2-0)
Tim Steele's excellent right-wing cross on 55 minutes looked far too deep but Nigel Vaughan kept the ball in play and quickly fed it back into the danger-zone where Bully's head did the rest...a looping header over the stranded Tony Parks.

115   12 April 1989 v. Torquay United (a) Sherpa Van Trophy, area Final, 1st leg (won 2-1)
Following Floyd Street's free-kick, substitute Mick Gooding (on for Phil Chard) found Bully with a crisp short pass.
Taking a few strides forward Bully whipped in a right-foot shot from 15 yards to bring Wolves level with four minutes remaining.

116   12 April 1989 v. Torquay United (a) Sherpa Van Trophy, area Final, 1st leg (won 2-1)
Amazingly, with time fast-running out, Dennison headed the ball forward. Mutch took out two defenders, allowing Bully to race through the centre to snatch the winning goal with a hammer-blow past Keith Veysey.

117   15 April 1989 v. Aldershot (a) League Division 3 (won 2-1).
In the 39th minute Mick Gooding was able to find enough space to squeeze a pass through the Aldershot defence for Bully to run onto, ahead of his markers. He finished in style with a left-footer past future Wolves' keeper Tony Lange.

118   1 May 1989 v. Bristol City (h) League Division 3 (won 2-0)
When Mutch flicked on Mick Gooding's 36th minute flighted pass, Bully seemed well off the pace but he quickly changed gear, got up speed, barged past Rob Newman and went on to beat Keith Waugh from a right-foot shot from just inside the area.

119   1 May 1989 v. Bristol City (h) League Division 3 (won 2-0)
With two minutes remaining, the alert Mutch clipped a short pass up to Bully who brought it down, turned and cracked a close range effort wide of Waugh.

120   6 May 1989 v. Northampton Town (h) League Division 3 (won 3-2)
In the 22nd minute Dennison found Gary Bellamy at the near post. In turn, he headed on to Bully who found the net with a powerful finish.

121   9 May 1989 v. Sheffield United (h) League Division 3 (drew 2-2)
After collecting Nigel Vaughan's pass out on the left, Andy Mutch whipped over a terrific cross which zipped over the 'keeper for Bully to head home his 50th goal of the season in the 42nd minute.

122   26 August 1989 v. Bradford City (h) League Division 2 (drew 1-1)
Robbie Dennison's quickly-taken free-kick on 69 minutes found Bully who darted in front of his marker to plant a cleverly directed header wide of Paul Tomlinson.

123 30 August 1989 v. Lincoln City (a) Littlewoods Cup, 1st round 2nd leg (won 2-0).
On 17 minutes, with nowhere to go and unable to see the framework of the goal, Bully somehow got in a left-footed shot which sped
through a ruck of players and past Andy Gorton into the net.

124 12 September 1989 v. Brighton & Hove Albion (h) League Division 2 (lost 2-4)
On the half-hour mark, Shane Wesley's knockdown inside the Albion penalty-area created panic and as a result Bully
somehow managed to scramble the ball into the net from close range.

125 26 September 1989 v. Barnsley (a) League Division 2 (drew 2-2)
Dennison's fine 38th minute cross was aimed for John Paskin and Nigel Vaughan; they both missed it, Bully didn't, following up near the
penalty-spot, to stab the ball left-footed into the net.

126 26 September 1989 v. Barnsley (a) League Division 2 (drew 2-2)
Eight minutes after half-time Bully was left clear to smash home a low drive after Malcolm Shotton had failed to clear Floyd Street's
long free-kick.

127 30 September 1989 v. Portsmouth (h) League Division 2 (won 5-0)
With 12 minutes left for play, Tom Bennett supplied the perfect through ball for Bully to run onto and score with
a fierce drive past Alan Knight.

128 30 September 1989 v. Portsmouth (h) League Division 2 (won 5-0)
Keith Downing's fine pass found Bully at the near post; his finish was exceptional, Knight having no hope of saving
his powerfully struck shot in the 68th minute.

129 4 October 1989 v. Aston Villa (h) Littlewoods Cup, 2nd round 2nd leg (drew 1-1)
Bully, despite seeing goalkeeper Nigel Spink charging out at him, somehow got his head to Nigel Vaughan's left-wing cross to find
the net in the 76th minute…seconds later he was being treated by the physio after a crunching collision.

130 15 October 11989 v. West Bromwich Albion (a) League Division 2 (won 2-1).
With the referee set to blow for full-time, Andy Mutch got in a right-wing cross. Bully pulled away from Chris Whyte,
chested the ball down and belted it on the half-volley into the net to give his side victory.

131 17 October 1989 v. Port Vale (h) League Division 2 (won 2-0).
On 34 minutes Shane Westley found Dennison whose inch-perfect cross was thrashed left-footed into the net by Bully.

132 4 November 1989 v. West Ham United (h) League Division 2 (won 1-0).
Played in by Mutch in the 66th minute, Bully outpaced centre-half Gary Strodder before firing in a shot at goal.
Hammers' 'keeper Phil Parkes who got his hand to the ball, couldn't prevent it crossing the line.

133 26 December 1989 v. Hull City (h) League Division 2 (lost 1-2)
After some superb work down the left by Mark Venus and Robbie Dennison, Bully finished off the move with a blistering close range
shot in the 20th minute to score his first goal for seven-and-a-weeks.

134 1 January 1990 v. Newcastle United (a) League Division 2 (won 4-1)
Following Paul Cook's excellent cross from the left, Bully opened his side's account at St James' Park in the 50th minute with
a near-post shot after a mistake by Bjorn Kristensen.

135 1 January 1990 v. Newcastle United (a) League Division 2 (won 4-1)
In the 56th minute Bully grabbed his second goal, stepping round former Wolves' keeper John Burridge after collecting
Keith Downing's through-ball.

136 1 January 1990 v. Newcastle United (a) League Division 2 (won 4-1)
Bully duly registered a nine-minute hat-trick when he headed home at the far post after Dennison's corner had been flicked
over the United defence.

137 1 January 1990 v. Newcastle United (a) League Division 2 (won 4-1)
Not too many visiting players score four goals at Newcastle - but Bully did, celebrating the New Year in style in the 76th minute when he
took Dennison's pass in his stride before skipping round Burridge to find the net with another smart left-footer.

Celebrating another goal...
this time against Birmingham City
on 17th November 1996

BULLY'S GOALS

138 6 January 1990 v. Sheffield Wednesday (h) FA Cup 3rd round (lost 1-2)
Wolves were awarded a 70th minute free-kick (for hand-ball) 25 yards inside the Wednesday half. Dennison picked out Bully
whose brilliant header beat Chris Turner low to his right

139 13 January 1990 v. Bradford City (a) League Division 2 (drew 1-1)
Chesting down Tom Bennett's measured right-wing cross, Bully moved forward a yard before rifling his shot beyond Paul Tomlinson
in the City goal to earn Wolves a point with just four minutes remaining.

140 10 February 1990 v. Ipswich Town (h) League Division 2 (won 2-1)
Paul Cook's well-struck corner was met at the far post by Bully, whose powerful header whizzed past 'keeper Forrest.

141 24 February 1990 v. Watford (h) League Division 2 (drew 1-1)
Some neat footwork out on the right by Paul McLoughlin saw the midfielder get the better of Jason Drysdale before sending over
a terrific cross which Bully, racing in at full pelt, headed home from eight yards to give Wolves a 13th minute lead.

142 6 March 1990 v. Portsmouth (a) League Division 2 (won 3-1)
Martin Kuhl's awful back-pass set Bully up for an easy last minute goal to tie up the victory.

143 10 March 1990 v. Barnsley (h) League Division 2 (drew 1-1)
Paul Cook delivered a beautiful 60th minute set piece from near the touchline and in swept Bully to plant a firm header low into the net
past 'keeper Clive Baker.

144 20 March 1990 v. West Bromwich Albion (h) League Division 2 (won 2-1)
Mark Kendall's clearance was collected and then moved on by Mutch to Bully who raced clear, rounded 'keeper Stuart Naylor and
netted from 10 yards for the 77th minute winner, thus clinching the double over Albion.

145 10 April 1990 v. Leicester City (h) League Division 2 (won 5-0)
In the seventh minute the ball squirted out of the City defence to Bully whose fierce 20-yard drive flew low into the net.

146 10 April 1990 v. Leicester City (h) League Division 2 (won 5-0)
In the 65th minute Bully brilliantly hooked in his second goal of the night after Nigel Vaughan and Andy Mutch had created
the opening with some deft footwork.

147 10 April 1990 v. Leicester City (h) League Division 2 (won 5-0)
Receiving Andy Thompson's quick throw-in on 70 minutes, Robbie Dennison squared the ball to Bully who glided in his
third right-footer of the match to secure yet another treble for Wolves.

148 21 April 1990 v. Oxford United (h) League Division 2 (won 2-0)
Steve Foster was left for dead in the 65th minute as Bully' raced on to beat 'keeper Alan Judge with a stunning right-foot shot
from fully 15 yards, the ball flying into the top far corner of the goal.

149 25 August 1990 v. Oldham Athletic (h) League Division 2 (lost 2-3)
Paul Cook delicately lofted a forward pass ahead of Bully who then went on to beat Jon Hallworth from 15 yards to open
the scoring on six minutes.

150 25 August 1990 v. Oldham Athletic (h) League Division 2 (lost 2-3)
Two minutes after half-time Bully scored his 150th goal for Wolves when he turned in Brian Roberts' deep cross at the far post
after Andy Thompson had made the initial drive forward.

151 28 August 1990 v. Port Vale (a) League Division 2 (won 2-1)
Bully's goal in the 42nd minute proved to be the winner. From Mike Stowell's clearance, he took Andy Mutch's short pass in his stride
and drove the ball home from just inside the area.

152 15 September 1990 v. West Ham United (a) League Division 2 (drew 1-1)
Paul Cook's split the Hammers' defence with a lovely angled pass, enabling Bully to control the ball before beating Ludek Miklosko
with a low drive from 15 yards.

153 22 September 1990 v. Plymouth Argyle (h) League Division 2 (won 3-1)
Again Paul Cook created the opening, which Bully executed supremely well in the 35th minute, netting from the corner of
the penalty area with a stunning shot across 'keeper Rhys Wilmot and into the net.

154 22 September 1990 v. Plymouth Argyle (h) League Division 2 (won 3-1)
Paul Cook's viciously struck right-wing corner was flicked on by Rob Hindmarch for Bully to bury his header at the far post
two minutes from half-time.

155 2 October 1990 v. Charlton Athletic (h) League Division 2 (won 2-0)
Robbie Dennison's in-swinging corner from the left was guided over 'keeper Mike Salmon's head by the purposeful Bully
in the 10th minute.

156 2 October 1990 v. Charlton Athletic (h) League Division 2 (won 2-0)
Bully secured the points with his second goal in injury-time...chasing after his own pass (from McLoughlin's neat through ball)
he controlled it, left two defenders foundering and then turned inside to bang a sweet right-footer into the net from 20 yards.

157 6 October 1990 v. Bristol City (h) League Division 2 (won 4-0)
Taking Gary Bellamy's through-ball in his stride, Bully raced on to drive a left-foot shot wide of City's on-rushing 'keeper Ronnie Sinclair
on 16 minutes.

158 6 October 1990 v. Bristol City (h) League Division 2 (won 4-0)
In the 67th minute Bully made it 3-0 to Wolves when he controlled Tim Steele's seemingly over-hit cross on his thigh
before beating Sinclair from close range.

159 6 October 1990 v. Bristol City (h) League Division 2 (won 4-0)
Cutting in past David Rennie in the 80th minute, Bully didn't hit his shot too well but 'keeper Sinclair made a hash of things,
allowing the ball to trickle through his hands and over the line.

160 20 October 1990 v. Hull City (a) League Division 2 (won 2-1).
In the 7th minute Robbie Dennison and Keith Downing contested Tim Steele's cross; 'keeper Iain Hesford flapped and Bully picked up
the pieces, scoring comfortably from five yards.

161 23 October 1990 v. Middlesbrough (h) League Division 2 (won 1-0)
Bully grabbed the deciding goal of this tight encounter on 61 minutes, gliding the ball sweetly past Stephen Pears
after Alan McLoughlin had intelligently flicked-on Keith Downing's splendid pass.

162 27 November 1990 v. Leicester City (a) Zenith Data Systems Cup, 1st round (won 1-0)
On 10 minutes Tim Steele raced down the right to collect Robbie Dennison's and his superb cross was cracked home past Mike Hooper.

163 1 December 1990 v. Ipswich Town (h) League Division 2 (drew 2-2)
Controlling Andy Thompson's 4th minute pass with his left foot, Bully turned on a sixpence before rifling home a shot with
his right from fully 20 yards.

164 1 December 1990 v. Ipswich Town (h) League Division 2 (drew 2-2)
With 12 minutes remaining Bully took Paul Cook's chipped pass in his stride before charging forward to smash the ball
past 'keeper Craig Forrest.

165 22 December 1990 v. Millwall (h) League Division 2 (won 4-1)
Robbie Dennison's low drive was saved by the diving Brian Horne but Bully was there to pick up the pieces, cracking the ball
high into the net from six yards.

166 26 December 1990 v. Sheffield Wednesday (a) League Division 2 (drew 2-2)
Paul Cook's splendid right-wing cross was headed home by Bully who stopped to make contact with the ball in the 84th minute
to earn his side a point after being 2-0 down at half-time.

167 12 January 1991 v. Brighton & Hove Albion (h) League Division 2 (lost 2-3)
In the 17th minute Andy Thompson's long throw was headed on by Bully to Andy Mutch who then fed the ball back to Bully
who hit the roof of the net with power from an acute angle.

168 2 February 1991 v. West Ham United (h) League Division 2 (won 2-1)
Andy Mutch latched onto Ian Bishop's poor pass, fed Bully who went to on to net what proved to be the winner in the 49th minute.

169 26 February 1991 v. Port Vale (h) League Division 2 (won 3-1).
Paul Cook to Mutch, a hard, low cross to Bully who scored from close range on 30 minutes.

170 26 February 1991 v. Port Vale (h) League Division 2 (won 3-1).
Another goal 'tailor-made' by Cook whose precise lob over a batch of defenders reached Bully's left foot…Vale 'keeper Mark Grew sniffed air as the ball flew into the net three minutes before half-time.

171 5 March 1991 v. Leicester City (h) League Division 2 (won 2-1)
Seeing Mike Stowell's 5th minute clearance misjudged by Tony James, Bully cashed in on the error, raced past Steve Walsh and shot at goal. Keeper Carl Muggleton saved but couldn't hold the ball, allowing Bully to run in and net with ease.

172 16 March 1991 v. Oxford United (h) League Division 2 (drew 3-3)
In the 11h minute, Paul Cook's supremely measured 30-yard pass was headed over 'keeper Ken Veysey by the raging Bully.

173 16 March 1991 v. Oxford United (h) League Division 2 (drew 3-3)
Five minutes later it was 2-0 as Bully' brilliantly headed home Andy Thompson's centre.

174 16 March 1991 v. Oxford United (h) League Division 2 (drew 3-3)
Steve Foster made a hash of his pass out of defence. Bully pounced, rounded Veysey and scored with aplomb with his left peg, claiming a hat-trick in 24 minutes - alas, to no avail!

175 30 March 1991 v. Sheffield Wednesday (h) League Division 2 (won 3-2)
Seemingly a yard or two offside when he received Andy Thompson's pass, Bully didn't ask any questions, slipping the ball home in the 70th minute.

176 17 August 1991 v. Watford (a) League Division 2 (won 2-0)
In the 71st minute Bully tied up the points with a neat header from Paul Cook's wonderful curling free-kick.

177 24 August 1991 v. Charlton Athletic (h) League Division 2 (drew 1-1)
In the 33rd minute Bully levelled the scores with a right-foot volley after bringing down and controlling a high cross when there seemed little danger!

178 31 August 1991 v. Brighton & Hove Albion (a) League Division 2 (drew 3-3)
Mark Venus's 33rd minute centre landed in between Albion defender Gary O'Reilly and Bully, but the Wolves man was strong enough to gain possession before beating Perry Digweed with a smart left-footer which sped low into the net.

179 7 September 1991 v. Oxford United (h) League Division 2 (won 3-1)
In the eighth minute Venus found Keith Downing whose ball over the head of Steve Foster was collected by Bully (after hesitation by Andy Melville) and from 15 yards the striker buried his shot beyond Veysey for his fourth goal against Oxford in two games.

180 14 September 1991 v. Newcastle United (a) League Division 2 (won 2-1)
Robbie Dennison's in-swinging corner on 73 minutes was flicked-on by Lawrie Madden for Bully to net from point-blank range.

181 17 September 1991 v. Cambridge United (a) League Division 2 (lost 1-2)
Faced with his second one-on-one situation of the game, this time Bully made no mistake, rounding 'keeper John Vaughan to score with ease on 76 minutes.

182 21 September 1991 v. Swindon Town (h) League Division 2 (won 2-1)
Moving forward onto Tom Bennett's 79th minute defence-splitting pass, Bully held off Colin Calderwood's challenge before flashing a rising drive past 'keeper Nicky Hammond.

183 24 September 1991 v. Shrewsbury Town (h) Rumbelows Cup, 2nd round 1st leg (won 6-1)
After the ball had bobbled around inside the 'Shrews' penalty-area Bullys strength allowed him to get the better of 'keeper Ken Hughes before scrambling it over the line for Wolves' fourth goal on the stroke of half-time.

Enjoying a friendly tussle with Wayne Jacobs and Peter Beagrie of Bradford City, May 1999.

184 24 September 1991 v. Shrewsbury Town (h) Rumbelows Cup, 2nd round 1st leg (won 6-1)
Four minutes after the break Bully whipped in goal number five, angling the ball home after Downing's shot had been
brilliantly turned aside by Hughes.

185 30 October 1991 v. Everton (a) Rumbelows Cup, 3rd round (lost 1-4)
On 22 minutes Paul Birch sent Mutch scurrying away down the flank and when his early cross was delivered Bully' was there to score
with a composed right-foot shot from near the penalty spot.

186 5 November 1991 v. Bristol Rovers (h) League Division 2 (lost 2-3)
Not expecting a shot, Rovers' 'keeper Tim Parkin was left floundering as Bullys 40th minute right-foot shot sped past him after
the striker had created an opening out of nothing from Mark Burke's cross.

187 5 November 1991 v. Bristol Rovers (h) League Division 2 (lost 2-3)
Taking Tom Bennett's 77th minute cross on hi chest. Bully let the ball drop before cracking it superbly with his right foot past 'keeper
Parkin. A great goal - it was pity that only 8,536 fans saw it!

188 21 December 1991 v. Port Vale (a) League Division 2 (drew 1-1)
Chasing hard into the Vale penalty area, Bully opened the scoring by firing home a crashing right-footer on 13 minutes.

189 15 January 1992 v. Charlton Athletic (a) League Division 2 (won 2-0)
Capitalising on some sloppy play by Steve Gatting, Paul Birch gained possession, fed Bully who banged home Wolves' opening goal
on 42 minutes.

190 18 January 1992 v. Watford (h) League Division 2 (won 3-0)
Mark Venus and Andy Thompson linked up well down the left on 76 minutes, and when the latter's cross came over,
Bully chested the ball down, drew back his foot and cracked it past Keith Waugh from 10 yards.

191 1 February 1992 v. Leicester City (h) League Division 2 (won 1-0)
Taking on and getting the better of four City defenders, Bully won the match for Wolves when, in a packed goalmouth,
he scored with a powerful low right-footed drive in the 36th minute.

192 8 February 1992 v. Tranmere Rovers (a) League Division 2 (lost 3-4)
Paul Birch swung over a 13th minute free-kick which was headed superbly past 'keeper Eric Nixon by Bully from eight yards.

193 7 March 1992 v. Bristol City (h) League Division 2 (drew 1-1)
On the stroke of half-time defender Russell Osman slipped, Bully pounced, collected Tom Bennett's chip and whipped in
a terrific shot past Keith Welch.

194 11 March 1992 v. Bristol Rovers (a) League Division 2 (drew 1-1)
Full-back Kevin Ashley delivered a wonderful right-wing cross which the unmarked Bully rose to head home in the 77th minute.

195 21 March 1992 v. Derby County (a) League Division 2 (won 2-1)
In the 73rd minute Andy Mutch dropped the ball into the County danger-zone; 'keeper Martin Taylor slipped,
Bully took control and nonchalantly lobbed the ball into the net from ten yards. It proved to be the winning goal.

196 31 March 11992 v. Newcastle United (h) League Division 2 (won 6-2)
With time running out and Wolves 5-2 in front, Bully finally got on the scoresheet with a rasping angled drive in the 87th minute -
as the United defence retreated under pressure.

197 14 April 1992 v. Blackburn Rovers (a) League Division 2 (won 2-1)
Derek Mountfield's long free-kick on 55 minutes was touched on by Andy Mutch to Bully who turned superbly before
smashing the ball right-footed past Rovers' debutant 'keeper Matt Dickens.

198 20 April 1992 v. Southend United (h) League Division 2 (won 3-1)
In the 37th minute 'Bully taking a neat pass from Keith Downing, turned and beat 'keeper Paul Sansome with a low angled
drive from a yard inside the penalty-area.

199 15 August 1992 v. Brentford (a) League Division 1 (won 2-0)
Racing into position on the right side of the penalty-area, Bully took Keith Downing's pass in his stride before booming a shot
past 'keeper Graham Benstead on 54 minutes.

200 18 August 1992 v. Leicester City (h) League Division 1 (won 3-0)
An appreciative crowd of 15,821 saw Steve Bully become the first Wolves player to score 200 goals in competitive football
(in his 295th game). Andy Thompson's pass was mis-headed, without conviction, by City defender Steve Walsh. The ball reached Bully
who chested it down before tucking past Carl Muggleton in the 19th minute.

201 5 September 1992 v. Peterborough United (h) League Division 1 (won 4-3)
In the sixth minute, Paul Cook's diagonal pass rebounded off Ronnie Robinson for Bully to pounce and steer his shot wide
of 'Posh 'keeper Ian Bennett.

202 19 September 1992 v. Watford (h) League Division 1 (drew 2-2)
In the 38th minute Bully rose highest to steer Paul Cook's curling free-kick into the net past the stranded 'keeper Perry Suckling
from close range.

203 19 September 1992 v. Watford (h) League Division 1 (drew 2-2)
With three minutes remaining and the Hornets 2-1 ahead, Bully came to the rescue when he nipped in to connect
with Robbie Dennison's low cross from the left.

204 22 September 1992 v. Notts County (a) Coca-Cola Cup, 2nd round 1st leg (lost 2-3)
After a smart 12th minute build-up involving Derek Mountfield and Andy Mutch, Bully hooked a left-foot shot past Steve Cherry
from eight yards.

205 30 September 1992 v. Peterborough United (h) Anglo-Italian Cup, Preliminary round (won 2-0)
A minute after half-time Paul Birch delivered a superb chipped ball over the defence. As it dropped over his right shoulder
Bully connected brilliantly to send his volleyed screaming into the net across the diving Ian Bennett.

206 7 November 1992 v. Bristol Rovers (h) League Division 1 (won 5-1)
On 28 minutes Paul Cook's headed pass split the Rovers defence. Robbie Dennison swung over a cross for Bully to race in
and send a right foot shot into the net past the advancing Tim Parkin.

207 7 November 1992 v. Bristol Rovers (h) League Division 1 (won 5-1)
In the 62nd minute Mark Burke swung over a neat cross from the right which Bully volleyed past Parkin first time with his left foot

208 14 November 1992 v. Notts County (a) League Division 1 (drew 2-2)
Burke was the provider, this time on 48 minutes. His sweetly timed right-wing cross into he inside-right channel,
found Bully who beat Steve Cherry at his near post.

209 5 December 1992 v. Cambridge United (a) League Division 1 (drew 1-1)
Right-back Kevin Ashley's forward pass on 79 minutes found 'Bully; alone just outside the penalty area. Appeals for offside
were ignored as the ball was volleyed home in style - a beauty.

210 2 January 1993 v. Watford (a) FA Cup 3rd round (won 4-1)
Bully rounded things off in the 86th minute with a simple tap-in from five yards after Paul Blades had dribbled round 'keeper Suckling
to set him up.

211 27 February 1993 v. Southend United (h) League Division 1 (drew 1-1)
In the 50th minute Paul Cook's intelligent through pass was collected by 'Bully;' who strode on before lobbing the ball
over 'keeper Paul Sansome's head.

212 6 March 1993 v. West Ham United (a) League Division 1 (lost 1-3)
In the 57th minute Mark Rankine created space down the left and his pull-back was cracked into the net, right-footed by the raging 'Bull.'

213 9 March 1993 v. Notts County (h) League Division 1 (won 3-0)
Bully broke the deadlock on 66 minutes when he capitalised on a mix-up between goalkeeper Cherry and defender Charlie Palmer
to snap up a gift from 10 yards.

214 9 March 1993 v. Notts County (h) League Division 1 (won 3-0)
Bully made it 3-0 with a minute to go. Burke, Cook and Mutch combined down the right and the former's cross to the far post
was headed firmly into the net.

215 13 March 1993 v. Bristol Rovers (a) League Division 1 (drew 1-1)
In the 7th minute, Robbie Dennison's splendid 30-yard pass was collected by Mutch who, after making ground, crossed to the far post for Bully to head in from six yards.

216 20 March 1993 v. Cambridge United (h) League Division 1 (lost 1-2)
Robbie Dennison's 66th minute corner was deflected into the crowded goalmouth where Bully stuck out his foot to guide the ball into the net.

217 7 April 1993 v. Luton Town (a) League Division 1 (drew 1-1)
With nine minute left on the watch Bully snatched an equaliser. After catching up with Mutch's pass, from a Mark Venus free-kick, he brushed aside defender John Dreyer and side-footed the ball through the mud past 'keeper Alex Chamberlain.

218 14 August 1993 v. Bristol City (h) League Division 1 (won 3-1)
Bully opened his account for the season in the ninth minute when hesitancy in centre-field, following a long clearance by Mike Stowell, allowed Kevin Keen to steer the ball into the striker who left three defenders for dead before smashing his shot into the roof of the net from 20 yards. A great goal.

219 14 August 1993 v. Bristol City (h) League Division 1 (won 3-1)
With five minutes remaining Bully secured victory when, with his left foot, he tucked away Kevin Keen's low cross with ease. This, in fact, was his 13th goal in games with City - the most he has ever netted against one specific club.

220 25 August 1993 v. Millwall (h) League Division 1 (won 2-0)
David Kelly had two bites at the cherry before crossing from the right for Bully to race in and score comfortably on 32 minutes.

221 31 August 1993 v. Stoke City (h) Anglo-Italian Cup Preliminary round (drew 3-3)
Paul Cook's 79th minute right-wing corner was cracked into the net by the unmarked Bully

222 5 September 1993 v. West Bromwich Albion (a) League Division 1 (lost 2-3)
In the 5th minute the unmarked Bully scored at the Brummie Road End with a neat header after some smart work by Paul Cook and a neat cross from Paul Birch.

223 2 November 1993 v. Notts County (h) League Division 1 (won 3-0)
With time running out and Wolves in charge Bully finally got on the scoresheet in the 86th minute when he smashed Kevin Keen's low cross into the net off the underside of the bar.

224 7 November 1993 v. Derby County (a) League Division 2 (won 4-0)
In the 18th minute Paul Birch split the County defence with a splendid ball, allowing Bully to race on and lob 'keeper Taylor from eight yards.

225 7 November 1993 v. Derby County (a) League Division 2 (won 4-0)
Paul Edwards' deep cross on the hour mark was headed back by David Kelly for Bully to crack into the net from eight yards.

226 7 November 1993 v. Derby County (a) League Division 2 (won 4-0)
This time a superb long ball from Edwards found Bully in the clear to head gleefully over Taylor to complete his hat-trick on 68 minutes.

227 27 November 1993 v. Leicester City (a) League Division 2 (drew 2-2)
In the 29th minute David Kelly flicked-on Kevin Keen's cross for Bully to nip in and send a splendid downward header into the net to the right of 'keeper Gavin Ward

228 27 November 1993 v. Leicester City (a) League Division 2 (drew 2-2)
five minutes Bully was there again, finishing off Paul Cook's inch-perfect through ball with a brilliant right-footed drive to the near post.

229 5 December 1993 v. Derby County (h) League Division 2 (drew 2-2)
On the stroke of half-time Bully - making his 300th appearance for the club - scored his fourth goal in a month against the Rams, clipping home the equaliser from close range after some smart build-up play through the middle.

230 12 December 1993 v. Watford (h) League Division 2 (drew 2-2)
On a slippery pitch, following a hail-storm, Bullys low 25-yarder (from Dennison's through ball in the 26th minute) skidded into the net as the Hornets' young 'keeper Simon Sheppard lost his footing at the crucial time.

July 1999, and it's during the Wolves pre-season tour of Sweden where the full impact of my knee problem was becoming apparent

231 27 December 1993 v. Tranmere Rovers (a) League Division 2 (drew 1-1)
Paul Cook's 62nd minute pass was headed in towards the penalty area by Neil Masters for Bully to smash right-footed past Eric Nixon from 15 yards.

232 3 May 1994 v. Sunderland (h) League Division 1 (drew 1-1)
In the 16th minute, Bully, brushing aside a stiff challenge from Kevin Ball, controlled Paul Cook's sweeping pass before smashing the ball home from 16 yards, giving 'keeper Tony Norman no chance whatsoever.

233 13 September 1994 v. Southend United (h) League Division 1 (won 5-0)
In the 68th minute Mike Stowell's throw-out found Steve Froggatt who galloped down the left before crossing to the far post where Bully netted via a post to make it 5-0.

234 17 September 1994 v. Burnley (a) League Division 1 (won 1-0)
The winning goal in the 59th minute came after Darren Ferguson's right-wing corner had been nodded on by David Kelly to Bully who couldn't believe his luck as he headed home from point-blank range.

235 20 September 1994 v. Chesterfield (a) Coca-Cola Cup 2nd round 1st leg (won 3-1)
Paul Birch and Darren Ferguson created the opening for Bully to roar in and level the scores on 63 minutes.

236 20 September 1994 v. Chesterfield (a) Coca-Cola Cup 2nd round 1st leg (won 3-1)
A great solo goal for Bully who raced away on a 40-yard dash before finishing with a thumping right-foot shot to sew up victory with five minutes remaining.

237 22 October 1994 v. Millwall (h) League Division 1 (drew 3-3)
Andy Thompson's long free-kick in the 27th minute was touched on by Mark Walters to Jamie Smith whose precise cross was header firmly into Kasey Keller's net by Bully

238 22 October 1994 v. Millwall (h) League Division 1 (drew 3-3)
Steve Froggatt's 53rd minute shot was fumbled by Keller, allowing Bully to sweep the ball into the net from close range.

239 30 October 1994 v. Stoke City (a) League Division 1 (drew 1-1)
In the 40th minute Bully snatched an equaliser for Wolves, cracking in shot from 18 yards when least expected.
Ex-Wolf Kevin Keen had given Stoke the lead.

240 10 December 1994 v. Notts County (h) League Division 1 (won 1-0)
The contest was decided 45 seconds after half-time. Jamie Smith crossed from the right and as the ball dropped Bully was there in a flash to sweep a right-foot shot into Steve Cherry's net

241 18 December 1994 v. Reading (a) League Division 2 (lost 2-4)
Bully scored on nine minutes with a smart header after some quick and skilful build-up which divided the Reading defence.

242 28 December 1994 v. Charlton Athletic (h) League Division 1 (won 2-0)
After missing a couple of easier chances early on, Bully found the net in the 38th minute with a close range header

243 25 February 1995 v. Port Vale (a) League Division 1 (won 4-2)
Right on half-time John de Wolf's forward pass found Don Goodman who flicked the ball to Bully whose lob over 'keeper Paul Musselwight was perfect.

244 5 March 1995 v. Portsmouth (h) League Division 1 (won 1-0)
Bully snatched an undeserved winner with 15 minutes remaining, his half-hit mis-shot squirting past 'Pompey' 'keeper Alan Knight at his near post.

245 24 March 1995 v. Burnley (h) League Division 1 (won 2-0)
Bully opened the scoring in the tenth minute with his right shin after 'Clarets' 'keeper Wayne Russell had misjudged the situation following David Kelly's lobbed pass.

246 1 April 1995 v. Southend United (a) League Division 1 (won 1-0)
A defence-splitting header by Don Goodman in the 83rd minute sent Bully charging through the centre. His shot was
beautifully clipped past the stranded Simon Royce.

247 15 April 1995 v. Charlton Athletic (a) League Division 1 (lost 2-3)
In the 43rd minute Bully connected sweetly with Gordon Cowans' left-wing cross to send the ball speeding past American 'keeper
Michael Amman.

248 15 April 1995 v. Charlton Athletic (a) League Division 1 (lost 2-3)
This time, on 66 minutes, a right-wing corner from Cowans found Bully whose header thudded into the net from eight yards.

249 22 April 1995 v. Sheffield United (a) League Division 1 (drew 3-3)
In a ding-dong contest Bully netted in the 65th minute, touching home a delightful left-wing cross from Mark Rankine.

250 3 May 1995 v. Tranmere Rovers (a) League Division 1 (drew 1-1)
Free inside the area, Bully collected Peter Shirtliff's 73rd minute pass before tucking away a right-foot shot past the advancing Eric Nixon

251 14 May 1995 v. Bolton Wanderers (h) Play-off semi-final, 1st leg (won 2-1)
Bully broke the deadlock a minute before half-time when he smashed the ball past veteran 'keeper Peter Shilton following
Robbie Dennison's excellent left-wing cross.

252 12 August 1995 v. Tranmere Rovers (a) League Division One (drew 2-2)
Bully opened his account for the season with a powerful header from Neil Masters' right-wing corner on 40 minutes.

253 9 September 1995 v. Grimsby Town (h) League Division 1 (won 4-1).
A delightful ball from Darren Ferguson picked out Bully inside the area. He went forward and beat 'keeper Paul Crichton from six yards
to give Wolves a 42nd minute equaliser.

254 9 September 1995 v. Grimsby Town (h) League Division 1 (won 4-1).
Bully pulling clear of hiss marker, collected Tony Daley's long pass and beat Crichton at his near post on 69 minutes.

255 28 October 1995 v. Sheffield United (h) League Division 1 (won 1-0)
Jermaine Wright found space and the angle to cross from the left and Bully powered home a header from seven yards
to win thee game on 37 minutes.

256 25 November 1995 v. Huddersfield Town (a) League Division 1 (lost 1-2)
A hopeful centre from Mark Atkins found Bully who sent a downward header through the legs of 'keeper Steve Francis from six yards
to reduce the deficit with 11 minutes remaining.

257 10 December 1995 v. Luton Town (a) League Division 1 (won 3-2)
Bully gave Wolves a 3-1 half-time lead when he rose, near the penalty-spot, to head in Darren Ferguson's pin-point free-kick
in the 41st minute.

258 26 December 1995 v. Millwall (h) League Division 1 (drew 1-1)
On 10 minutes Wolves were ahead. Taking Vinny Samways pass on his chest, Bully turned before cracking a fierce right-footer
low past Kasey Keller from 12 yards

259 30 December 1995 v. Portsmouth (h) League Division 1 (drew 2-2)
A 5th minute shot from Mark Atkins was blocked by 'keeper Alan Knight but Bully reacted quickest to clip the ball home,
right-footed, from five yards.

260 6 January 1996 v. Birmingham City (a) FA Cup 3ard round (drew 1-1)
A poor clearance by right-back Gary Poole struck Don Goodman and bounced nicely for Bully who timed his jump perfectly
to head home on 25 minutes.

261 17January 1996 v. Birmingham City (h) FA Cup 3rd round replay (won 2-1)
Bully scored the winning goal out of nothing. In the 62nd minute he tried a wild shot at goal. The ball took a deflection off
Michael Johnson and flew into the net past the stranded Bart Griemink

BULLY'S GOALS

262 20 January 1996 v. Tranmere Rovers (h) League Division 1 (won 2-1)
In the 35th minute Darren Ferguson surged forward, fed Simon Osborn whose quick cross was drilled home right-footed by Bully
to put his side ahead (1-0).

263 17 February 1996 v. Norwich City (a) League Division 1 (won 3-2)
Bully set the ball rolling with the game's opening goal on 12 minutes, lobbing 'keeper Bryan Gunn from 30 yards after Steve Corica
had robbed Ian Crook in midfield.

264 17 February 1996 v. Norwich City (a) League Division 1 (won 3-2)
Bully brought Wolves level at 2-2 on 37 minutes when he raced clear of a square defence to slot the ball past Gunn
with the outside of his right foot from 12 yards.

265 21 February 1996 v. Leicester City (h) League Division 1 (lost 2-3)
In the 26th minute City 'keeper Kevin Poole failed to hold Simon Osborn's cross-shot and Bully accepted the gift by smashing the ball
home from six yards.

266 2 March 1996 v. Millwall (a) League Division 1 (won 1-0)
Former Millwall player Neil Emblen set Bully up for his 6th minute, the striker delicately chipping the ball over Kasey Keller from 15 yards.

267 23 March v. Birmingham City (h) League Division 1 (won 3-2)
Bully scored his third goal of the season against Blues with a minute to go. He chased after Simon' defence-splitting pass to
angle a drive past 'keeper Bart Griemink from 20 yards to win the derby.

268 8 April 1996 v. Barnsley (h) League Division 1 (drew 2-2)
A poor back pass by Arjan De Zeeuw was pounced upon by Don Goodman who switched the ball to Bully who scored comfortably
from 10 yards to bring the scores level at 1-1 on 16 minutes.

269 17 August 1996 v. Grimsby Town (a) League Division 1 (won 3-1)
Steve Froggatt crossed from the left and Bully finding space clipped the ball into the net from eight yards to give Wolves
a 36th minute lead.

270 17 August 1996 v. Grimsby Town (a) League Division 1 (won 3-1)
Right on half-time Bully controlled Froggatt's downfield pass, and stroked a low shot wide of the advancing Jason Pearcey.

271 17 August 1996 v. Grimsby Town (a) League Division 1 (won 3-1)
Bully completed his hat-trick in the 70th minute when he shot home from eight yards after Froggatt had done the donkey-work

272 24 August 1996 v. Bradford City (h) League Division 1 (won 1-0)
With 18 minutes left on the watch, Dean Richards nodded down Osborn's left-wing free-kick for Bully to put away a right foot shot
from six yards.

273 15 September 1996 v. West Bromwich Albion (a) League Division 1 (won 4-2)
In the 14th minute Steve Froggatt's throw-in from the left was flicked on by Iwan Roberts for Bully to stab over the line
from five yards , giving his side a 2-0 lead.

274 13 October 1996 v. Southend United (a) League Division 1 (drew 1-1)
On 73 minutes Mark Venus and Glen Crowe played a one-two down the left and when the former's cross came over Bully;
was there to thump a header past Simon Royce from 16 yards to earn his side a point.

275 15 October 1996 v. Portsmouth (a) League Division 1 (won 2-0)
In the 12th minute Froggatt swung over a lefrt0-wing corner for the unmarked 'Bully;' to score with a six-yard header.

276 15 October 1996 v. Portsmouth (a) League Division 1 (won 2-0)
Bully tied things up on 68 minutes when he latched onto Russell Perrett's poor back pass, raced away and tucked the ball
with ease past 'keeper Aaron Flahavan.

277 27 October 1996 v. Manchester City (a) League Division 1 (won 1-0)
Bully stunned the home fans in the near 27,300 crowd by scoring the winner in the 76th minute. Picking up Dennis Pearce's through
ball he raced past Kit Symons before finding the net with a powerful right-footer from 20 yards past 'keeper Andy Dibble.

STEVE
BULL
WOLVES

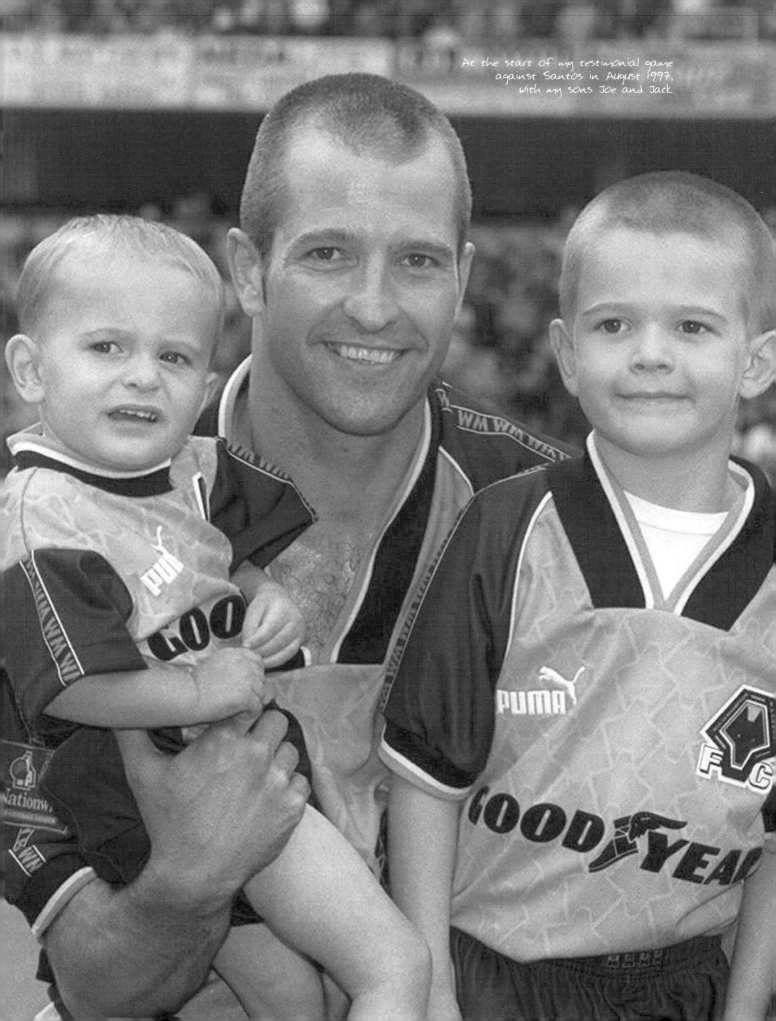

At the start of my testimonial game against Santos in August 1997, with my sons Joe and Jack

278 2 November 1996 v. Barnsley (h) League Division 1 (drew 3-3)
Bully brought Wolves back into the game at 3-2 in the 60th minute when he was on hand to bundle the ball into the net
from close range after 'keeper David Watson had missed Mark Venus' low cross.

279 17 November 1996 v. Birmingham City (h) League Division 2 (lost 1-2)
Again Bully found the net against Blues, but this time to no avail. He scored in the 9th minute after rounding 'keeper Ian Bennett
following Osborn's delightful through pass.

280 21 December 1996 v. Tranmere Rovers (a) League Division 1 (won 2-0)
In the 5th minute Don Goodman challenged Shaun Teale on the edge of the Rovers penalty-area and as the ball broke free,
so Bully let fly with his right foot to send a rocket past 'keeper Danny Coyne.

281 24 January 1997 v. Sheffield United (a) League Division 1 (won 3-2)
Bully won the game for Wolves in the 88th minute when he chased after Adrian Williams' pass before drawing Alan Kelly off his line
and then coolly slotting the ball into the net.

282 29 January 1997 v. Swindon Town (h) League Division 1 (won 1-0)
Neil Emblen's 34th minute cross was flicked-on by Don Goodman for Bully who finished in style with a rasping left footed drive
from 12 yards.

283 1 February 1997 v. Stoke City (h) League Division 1 (Won 2-0)
Steve Froggatt's pin-point free-kick on 12 minutes was headed home by Bully from near the penalty spot.

284 1 February 1997 v. Stoke City (h) League Division 1 (Won 2-0)
Another measured cross, this time by Neil Emblen on 54 minutes, was headed firmly past hapless 'keeper Carl Muggleton
by the dangerous Bully

285 8 February 1997 v. Huddersfield Town (a) League Division 1 (won 2-0)
Bully made the game safe for Wolves when, in the 84th minute, he robbed Jon Dyson, took the ball forward and drive it hard
past 'keeper Steve Francis who got a hand to it - that's all.

286 22 February 1997 v. Barnsley (a) League Division 1 (won 3-1)
After some sloppy defensive play and a bit of luck Bully lashed in his 18th goal of the season in the 99th second.

287 4 March 1997 v. Birmingham City (a) League Division 1 (won 2-1)
Once again Bully netted against Blues, this time after just 55 seconds. Steve Corica sent him racing clear and he made no mistake
with a deft finish past the non-rushing Ian Bennett.

288 8 March 1997 v. Tranmere Rovers (h) League Division 1 (won 3-2)
Bully edged Wolves in front on 34 minutes when he pounced on a weak back-pass from John McGreal to lob 'keeper Eric Nixon
from 12 yards.

289 8 March 1997 v. Tranmere Rovers (h) League Division 1 (won 3-2)
Five minutes before half-time Bully made it 2-0 when he raced onto a through ball and steered a smart ground shot
past Nixon from 14 yards.

290 15 March 1997 v. Oldham Athletic (a) League Division 1 (lost 2-3)
Bully equalised for Wolves (1-1) with a 23rd minute headed from six yards after Don Goodman had flicked the ball across goal
from the left.

291 19 April 1997 v. Southend United (h) League Division 1 (won 4-1)
After more than a month without a goal Bully got back on track with Wolves' second on nine minutes. Darren Ferguson's corner
was only partially cleared and the Wolves striker took full advantage with a smart header that went in off a post.

292 30 August 1997 v. Bury (h) League Division 1 (won 4-2)
Wolves went 2-1 in front on 42 minutes. Carl Robinson's long pass was collected by substitute Jermaine Wright
whose centre was converted in the run from six yards by 'Bully.'

293 30 August 1997 v. Bury (h) League Division 1 (won 4-2)
Six minutes into the second-half Bully was on target again, this time heading home Steve Froggatt's excellent cross from the left.

294 3 September 1997 v. Port Vale (h) League Division 1 (drew 1-1)
Bully produced another vintage goal when in the 74th minute he struck with a low shot from the edge of the area to put Wolves in front.

295 13 September 1997 v. Charlton Athletic (h) League Division 1 (won 3-1)
Bully opened the scoring in the 9th minute when he steered home Robbie Keane's right-wing cross at the near post.

296 13 September 1997 v. Charlton Athletic (h) League Division 1 (won 3-1)
Bully made it 3-0 in the33rd minute when Finnish international Mixu Paatelainen, receiving from Ferguson, fed a delightful pass into his path which the striker finished off in style.

297 27 September 1997 v. Huddersfield Town (h) League Division 1 (drew 1-1)
With the Huddersfield defence spread and unprepared Bully, picking up a loose ball, lashed in an 18 yard-snap shot to open the scoring inside the first minute.

298 14 October 1997 v. Reading (a) League Division 1 (lost 2-4)
A minute before half-time Bully pulled a goal back for Wolves (1-2) when he rose to head home Darren Ferguson's deep cross at the far post.

299 14 October 1997 v. Reading (a) League Division 1 (lost 2-4)
Bully made it 2-4 when, on 58 minutes, he forced the ball in from eight yards after 'keeper Steve Mautone had failed to gather Paatelainen's free-kick.

300 18 February 1998 v. Bradford City (h) League Division 1 (won 2-1
Bullys first goal for four months arrived in the final minute to earn Wolves victory. He stooped low to nod home Paul Simpson's piercing left-wing cross.

301 15 August 1998 v. Oxford United (a) League Division 1 (won 2-0)
On the half-time whistle Bully pounced after a right-wing cross from Kevin Muscat had been dropped by 'keeper Phil Whitehead who had been fairly in the air challenged by the Wolves striker.

302 18 August 1998 v. Barnet (h) Worthington Cup 1st round 2nd leg (won 5-0)
Exchanging passes with Robbie Keane, Bully surged into the penalty area on 14 minutes to meet the Irishman's low cross with a stooping header at the far post.

303 18 August 1998 v. Barnet (h) Worthington Cup 1st round 2nd leg (won 5-0)
Keane sent the Spaniard Fernando Gomez clear and from his cross, Bully controlled the ball on his chest before cracking it right-footed past the exposed 'keeper Lee Harrison from six yards.

304 18 August 1998 v. Barnet (h) Worthington Cup 1st round 2nd leg (won 5-0)
Bully completed the last hat-trick of his distinguished career in the 80th minute when he rose hard and shoulders above a tiring Barnet defence to nod home Steve Froggatt's corner.

305 28 August 1998 v. Watford (a) League Division 1 (won 2-0)
Bullys last away goal is his Football League career came in the 44th minute at Vicarage Road. He took Steve Froggatt's pass in his stride, cut in from the right side of the penalty area and then curled a superb 12yard shot round 'keeper Alex Chamberlain and into the Hornets' net.

306 26 September 1998 v. Bury (h) League Division 1 (won 1-0)
Bullys last-ever goal at senior level was scored in front of more than 20,000 fans at Molineux. It arrived halfway through the second-half when Kevin Muscat, on then overlap down the right, took Gomez's pass in his stride before sending over the perfect cross for the Wolves striker to plant a firm low header past Dean Kiely at the far post.

For Hereford United

1   17 February 2001 v. Nuneaton Borough (h) Nationwide Conference (drew 1-1)
Jon Snape's last minute cross was met at the far post by Bullys head to earn United a share of the spoils.

2   28 April 2001 v. Morecambe (h) Nationwide Conference (drew 2-2)
United, 2-1 down with five remaining, salvaged a point when Bully, collecting a through pass after some fine build-up play involving Elms and Giddings, rifled home a right foot shot from the edge of the area past 'keeper Smith.

For England

1   25 April 1989 v. Albania (h) European Under-21 championship (won 2-0)
In the 47th minute Bully found space inside the penalty area before turning on Steve Sedgley's exquisite pass to smash a right footer past the Albanian 'keeper. and around 200 Wolves supporters were delighted!

2   19 May 1989 v. Iceland (a) 'B' international (won 2-0)
In freezing conditions Bully - on as an early second-half substitute - raced forward, shrugged off a defender and then fired home an unstoppable shot from 12 yards to clinch victory.

3   22 May 1989 v. Norway (a) 'B' international (won 1-0)
A rare penalty - fired home nonchalantly in the 61st minute after nobody wanted to take the responsibility. A goal-bound shot from Albion's Tony Ford was handled by the Norwegian defender Hansen. Bully placed the ball on the spot and smacked it straight and high into the roof of the net.

4   27 May 1989 v. Scotland (a) Rous Cup - full international (won 2-0)
With 10 minutes remaining and England 1-0 ahead through Chris Waddle's goal, right-back Gary Stevens propelled a high cross towards the penalty spot. Bully jumped with defender Dave McPherson only for the ball to hit him on the shoulder and spin up into the air. Before anyone else reacted Bully was on to it in a flash and as it dropped, he struck it with his right foot and the ball flew like a rocket past Jim Leighton in the Scotland goal.

5   10 October 1989 v. Poland (a) European Under-21 championship (won 3-1)
With defenders worrying about his presence, Bully roared in to send a powerful header into the net from eight yards.

6   10 October 1989 v. Poland (h) European Under-21 championship (won 3-1)
Bully doubled his account with a well struck right foot shot from just inside the penalty area after a neat build-up involving Paul Ince, Paul Merson and Alan Smith.

7   25 April 1990 v. Czechoslovakia (h) Friendly international (won 4-0)
In the 18th minute Paul Gascoigne hit a wonderful long pass up to Bully who controlled the ball and then took it on a stride before smashing it past 'keeper Ludek Miklosko in the Czech goal.

8   25 April 1990 v. Czechoslovakia (h) Friendly international (won 4-0)
Gascoigne was again the creator with an excellent 50th minute right-wing cross which Bully, free from his marker, powered into the net with a close range header.

9   2 June 1990 v. Tunisia (a) Friendly international (drew 1-1)
With time fast running out and England staring defeat in the face, Gascoigne fed John Barnes out on the left wing. He found enough space to cross the ball into the centre. Bully raced forward, got a yard on two defenders, to steer the ball into the net at the near post with a stooping header.

I've got my eye on the ball against Belgium during the World Cup campaign in Italy 1990

GOAL TALK

The club sides Bully has scored against at competitive level:

For Albion:

Derby County	1
Ipswich Town	2
Total 3	

For Wolves:

Aldershot	2
Aston Villa	1
Barnet	3
Barnsley	6
Birmingham City	7
Blackburn Rovers	1
Blackpool	1
Bolton Wanderers	5
Bournemouth	2
Bradford City	4
Brentford	6
Brighton & Hove Albion	3
Bristol City	13
Bristol Rovers	6
Burnley	3
Bury	6
Cambridge United	4
Cardiff City	5
Carlisle United	1
Charlton Athletic	9
Cheltenham Town	3
Chester City	1
Chesterfield	2
Colchester United	1
Crewe Alexandra	1
Darlington	3
Derby County	5
Everton	1
Exeter City	5
Fulham	3
Gillingham	2
Grimsby Town	5
Hartlepool United	6
Hereford United	5
Huddersfield Town	5
Hull City	2
Ipswich Town	3
Leicester City	10
Leyton Orient	3
Lincoln City	3
Luton Town	2
Manchester City	2
Mansfield Town	4
Middlesbrough	1
Millwall	6
Newcastle United	6
Newport County	2
Northampton Town	1
Norwich City	2
Notts County	11
Oldham Athletic	3
Oxford United	6
Peterborough United	6
Plymouth Argyle	2
Port Vale	13
Portsmouth	7
Preston North End	4
Reading	3
Rochdale	1
Scarborough	1
Scunthorpe United	3
Sheffield United	4
Sheffield Wednesday	3
Shrewsbury Town	2
Southend United	8
Stockport County	4
Stoke City	4
Sunderland	1
Swansea City	5
Swindon Town	2
Torquay United	4
Tranmere Rovers	9
Watford	8
West Bromwich Albion	4
West Ham United	4
Wigan Athletic	1
Total: 306	

For Hereford United:

Morecambe	1
Nuneaton Borough	1
Total: 2	

Distribution of Goals

For Albion: Home 2, Away 1
For Wolves: Home 193, Away 113
For Hereford: Home 2
For England: Home 4, Away 5

* He also scored on almost 60 different Football League grounds.

Hat-Tricks

Bully scored 18 hat-tricks - all for Wolves - in four different competitions against 17 different clubs:

May 1987 League (h)	v. Hartlepool United (3)
Nov 1987 FA Cup (h)	v. Cheltenham Town (3)
Jan 1988 SVT (h)	v. Brentford (3)
Feb 1988 League (a)	v. Exeter City (3)
Mar 1988 League (h)	v. Darlington (3)
Nov 1988 League (h)	v. Preston North End (4)
Dec 1988 SVT (h)	v. Port Vale (4)
Dec 1988 League (h)	v. Mansfield Town (3)
Jan 1989 SVT (h)	v. Bristol City (3)
Feb 1989 League (h)	v. Fulham (3)
Mar 1989 League (h)	v. Bury (3)
Jan 1990 League (away)	v. Newcastle United (4)
Apr 1990 League (h)	v. Leicester City (3)
Oct 1990 League (h)	v. Bristol City (3)
Mar 1991 League (h)	v. Oxford United (3)
Nov 1993 League (away)	v. Derby County (3)
Aug 1996 League (away)	v. Grimsby Town (3)
Aug 1998 League Cup (home)	v. Barnet (3)

STEVE
BULL
My Memories of
WOLVES